Outlast

Outlast

The Hidden Power of Emotional Patience in Building Enduring Wealth How staying calm beats getting rich quick

Jonathan Mercer

Mindful Pages

Published in 2025

ISBN: 9789371771160 (PB)
ISBN: 9789371772754 (eBook)

Published by

Mindful Pages
Imprint of Alpha Editions LLC
312 W. 2nd St #1834
Casper, WY 82601, USA

This book was developed using advanced writing tools to support the drafting and ideation process. All content has been thoughtfully curated, refined, and reviewed to ensure quality and relevance.

Content

Introduction
The Invisible Engine of Wealth: Why Patience Outperforms Hustle

Wealth, in its truest and most durable form, has never been a race. It has always been a discipline—an invisible framework constructed not through frantic effort but by restraint, endurance, and the steady passage of time. Yet our culture insists otherwise.

The prevailing narrative urges us to hurry. Pivot. Hustle. Disrupt. Outperform in real time or risk irrelevance. The modern economy, with its endless slogans of acceleration, insists that fortune belongs only to the fast. From the slick promises of financial influencers selling instant prosperity to the jittery thrill of trading apps designed to mimic slot machines, we are told that the clock is the enemy. The unspoken warning is blunt: slow means failure.

But what if that story is not simply flawed, but reversed?

This work advances a different thesis: the most overlooked driver of enduring wealth is not speed, but patience. Not passive waiting, but an active, resilient patience—the kind that holds firm when others panic, that thinks in decades when others live in days. Far from weakness, it is a form of power: the compounding strength of those who can resist the incessant demand for immediacy.

Historically, patience has been treated as a moral virtue. Rarely has it been framed as a financial instrument. And yet, every fortune of substance—whether dynasties of antiquity or the portfolios of modern investors—rests upon it. Patience is the capacity to delay gratification, resist impulse, endure volatility. It is not softness, but strength at rest.

The Delusion of Speed in Wealth Creation

The idolisation of speed is no accident. It has been cultivated.

Technology has rewoven the rhythm of life. Social feeds refresh in moments, news cycles collapse into hours, and algorithms judge value in fractions of a second. Every industry is bent toward acceleration—of communication, consumption, speculation. And so expectations warp: what once demanded ten years must now be delivered in one; what once required mastery is replaced with mere access.

This obsession with velocity bleeds into our handling of money. Start-ups chase capital at breakneck pace. Crypto tokens mint millionaires overnight—and strip them just as quickly. Gurus peddle "systems" that dangle rewards without effort, returns without patience. The slow logic of compounding has been traded for the adrenaline rush of speculation.

But outcomes betray the myth. Lottery winners collapse under their winnings. High-frequency traders flame out. Trend-chasers underperform the very markets they try to outsmart. Behind the dazzling headlines of overnight triumph are the quieter, less glamorous stories: families who build across generations, investors who hold through decades, builders who endure storms. Their stories are harder to package, for they unfold too slowly for the news cycle. Yet they are the bedrock of dynasties.

The Emotional Economy: Why Resilience Matters Most

Strip wealth down to its essence and one question remains: who are you when nothing is happening?

Do you unravel in stillness? Do you move for the sake of moving? Or can you hold steady when the world grows restless?

Most assume financial outcomes hinge on timing, access, or specialised knowledge. In truth, the more consistent divider is internal: emotional resilience. The ability to remain calm amid discomfort. To hold a position through fear. To wait through the valleys instead of lunging at the first hilltop.

We are not merely rational economic beings; we are emotional ones. Our relationship with uncertainty dictates much of our relationship with wealth. The human brain, wired for immediacy and hyper-attuned to threat, is ill-suited for modern markets. It is not weakness, but biology. What instinct does not optimise, discipline can teach.

Resilience is therefore not abstract philosophy; it is investable capital. And patience is its most practical expression. Like financial capital, it compounds. It shields us from ruin, sustains us through decline, and allows us to make choices aligned with horizons far longer than our impulses allow.

Redefining Wealth: Less About Earnings, More About Endurance

Wealth has for too long been reduced to a tally of earnings, possessions, or outward displays. Yet lasting wealth—wealth that outlives markets, families, even lifetimes—is not about what is acquired, but about what is endured.

Picture two investors. Their portfolios are identical at the start. One reacts to every headline, sells at each dip, jumps strategies when the winds shift. The other holds firm, filters noise, and trusts in time. After years, the difference is staggering. Not because one had more insight, but because one had the capacity to do less. To endure.

The pattern echoes beyond money. Entrepreneurs who refuse distraction build resilient companies. Artists who ignore quick validation produce work of lasting consequence. Parents who model restraint raise children with depth and steadiness.

The common thread is philosophical: progress is not always motion. Urgency is not importance. Speed is not wealth.

What This Book Will Teach You

Outlast is not an argument against ambition, but for its sustainability. Ambition that burns itself out is no triumph. Across its chapters, this book will show you how to cultivate the most undervalued resource of the age: emotional patience.

You will discover how the architecture of your own brain—particularly the dopamine and fear circuits—shapes impulsive choices unless consciously retrained. You will encounter timeless traditions, from Stoicism to Taoism, offering tools for steadiness in volatile times. You will study case studies of investors, builders, and creators who have thrived not through speed but through constancy.

Here patience becomes visible as emotional capital: an asset as real as money itself. You will learn to treat volatility not as an enemy but as a tutor, and to reframe your financial and personal horizons accordingly.

The aim is practical. Mental models, strategies, and daily disciplines will be provided to reshape your response to uncertainty. But the larger goal is subtler: to rewire your sense of time itself. The emotionally wealthy do not think faster. They think further.

Why Now?

We live in an age thick with noise. The loudest voices carry the least wisdom. Speed masquerades as clarity. Yet beneath the surface, a recognition grows: the old gospel of hustle is hollow. True wealth requires stillness. What we endure, not what we seize, ultimately defines us.

This book is a part of that shift. Not a system, not a secret, but an invitation: from reaction to reflection, from immediacy to longevity, from hustle to patience.

The stakes are not theoretical. Our finances, our careers, our families, even our health now depend on how well we manage emotional volatility in an unstable world. Without patience, we repeat the cycle of bubbles and burnout. With it, we build something rare: wealth that is steady, resilient, enduring.

To outlast is to unlock this quiet strength. It begins, paradoxically, not with action, but with stillness. To build what matters, one must first learn to wait.

Chapter 1
The Speed Trap: How Modern Culture Hijacks Our Wealth Instincts

Once, affluence was measured not by the speed of acquisition but by what could be safeguarded and sustained. Land passed through generations, businesses tended with patience, capital that grew quietly through compounding restraint—these were the old signals of wealth. Today the signs have shifted. Wealth is no longer a discreet foundation but a performance: broadcast, tallied, and optimised for spectacle. Headlines churn with tales of instant fortunes, reinforcing the illusion that to stand still is to fall behind. The sense of urgency runs so deep it no longer feels external; it has embedded itself into our thinking, shaping how we approach money, risk, and even our sense of time.

This distortion is not an accident. It is carefully constructed by the platforms and ideologies that mediate modern life. Algorithms reward immediacy and emotion. Financial news spins out a daily theatre of shocks. Trading apps blur the line between empowerment and agitation, gently nudging users towards compulsive action. Career advice, filtered through the creed of hustle, insists that sleep is indulgence and rest a defect of character. The combined effect is to make calmness indistinguishable from idleness, and patience to appear as weakness masquerading as virtue.

At the root of it all is a profound misinterpretation of time. Volatility is constant, narratives are fleeting, and so our horizons contract. We make decisions meant for decades with the mentality of weeks, then demand lifetime outcomes from quarterly results. The contradiction is impossible to miss: we are using short-term tools to pursue long-term goals, undermining the very futures we claim to desire.

This chapter is an excavation of that paradox. It traces how our instincts about value, risk, and time have been systematically hijacked by a culture addicted to immediacy. It reveals how the architecture of urgency corrodes disciplined thinking. It critiques hustle culture—

not to dismiss diligence, but to expose how the modern form of "always on" often conceals restlessness, fear, and impulsive choices that rarely endure. It weighs the emotional and financial toll of chasing the latest frenzy: not only the loss of capital, but the erosion of clarity, intention, and composure. What vanishes, in the end, is our resilience and our strategic patience.

Take the meme-stock saga of 2021. GameStop's meteoric rise, powered by retail investors gathering on Reddit, was framed as a populist revolt against Wall Street. Yet behind the drama was a fragile dynamic: thousands entering the market on narrative alone, with no foundation beyond the thrill of collective defiance. Many rode the wave not with strategies or time-bound theses but with the intoxicating rush of a digital uprising. Some walked away with windfalls, many more with losses, and almost all with a sharper sense of regret. What lingered was a reinforced suspicion that investing is little more than roulette.

Episodes like this are not exceptions; they are symptoms. They signal a deeper cultural condition: our discomfort with stillness. Modern platforms coax us to act, refresh, buy, sell, move—anything but wait. Yet durable wealth, like robust health or strong character, is rarely born of frantic reaction. It is built in the slower, steadier decisions that resist glamour precisely because they lack drama.

The wider economic backdrop amplifies the pull of speed. Inflation, unaffordable housing, widening inequality—these pressures heighten the appeal of a shortcut. For someone under the weight of stagnant wages or student loans, the dream of a fast escape is not mere greed but survival. In this climate, hustle culture functions almost like a secular faith, promising empowerment and identity in a system that often feels unyielding. But like all faiths built on false premises, it cannot bear its own contradictions.

It is important to be precise here. The word "hustle" once meant initiative, persistence, a willingness to toil. Those qualities remain valuable. Hustle culture, however, has mutated into a doctrine of endless motion—an economy of insecurity disguised as productivity. It glorifies maximisation, visibility, the commodification of every waking hour. Morning routines are monetised, hobbies turned into side businesses, leisure reframed as laziness unless it earns. The results are plain enough: burnout surges, financial unease persists, freedom always seems postponed.

The damage is not confined to individuals. Businesses built on this ethos chase growth heedlessly, sacrificing resilience, only to collapse when conditions shift. Investors addicted to immediacy chronically underperform. A Dalbar study in 2022 showed that average investors earn consistently less than the markets themselves—not from ignorance, but from impulsive timing errors. The problem is not lack of data; it is a distorted sense of time. When years of strategy collapse into moments of panic or euphoria, both capital and patience lose their compounding power.

At the heart of all this lies the most seductive illusion of modern finance: the belief that faster is always better. And yes, in certain domains—technology, logistics—speed creates advantage. But in building wealth, velocity more often breeds fragility. Hasty decisions, made under duress, are less likely to align with the goals that truly matter. Patience, by contrast, creates margin. It grants the space to ask better questions, to analyse without frenzy, to act with clarity rather than fear.

Still, patience is not an accident of personality. It requires design. Systems, routines, and mental frameworks must support it. That means cultural resistance. It means reclaiming the right to wait when everything around you shouts for haste. It means recognising that deliberate stillness is not sloth but strategy.

This chapter is a call to that reclamation. It will explore the mechanics of urgency—from advertising engineered to spark fear of missing out, to platforms designed around intermittent rewards, to narratives that equate busyness with meaning. It will unpack the cognitive traps we fall into: mistaking noise for signal, volatility for opportunity, motion for progress. It will revisit the psychology of speculation—not in moral terms, but as a form of mental expenditure that leaves us poorer in judgement.

To outlast in today's economy is to resist the gravitational pull of speed. It is to choose a worldview where time is not an adversary but an ally. Where consistency, not thrill, provides satisfaction. Where the boldest act is not chasing the next surge, but having the discipline to hold steady for what endures.

There are no quick fixes here. No hacks to turn patience into a morning routine. What is offered instead is clarity: about how our environments warp instinct, and how we might recover the inner architecture for durability. If you find yourself overstimulated by choice, pressed by progress, unsettled by pace, you are not failing; you are inhabiting a system that thrives on your urgency. The remedy is not to sprint harder. It is to step back, slow the tempo, and reclaim your time.

Lasting wealth begins here—not with speed, but with stillness. Not with restless ambition, but with the patience to endure.

The Illusion of Urgency

If there is one defining trait of contemporary economic life, it is acceleration. Decisions that once spanned months are now made in minutes. Products are marketed, purchased, and discarded before the ink of their branding has dried. From financial markets to professional careers, the expectation is not only that we move—but that we move fast. This cultural tempo has generated a powerful illusion: that speed equates to intelligence, that urgency implies importance, and that decisive action is always preferable to patient inaction. But this belief—though emotionally compelling—is intellectually and economically hazardous. It distorts judgment, rewards reactivity over rigour, and undermines the very foundation upon which enduring wealth is built: emotional and temporal stability.

At the core of this illusion is a sophisticated ecosystem designed to hijack human attention. Marketing departments do not merely sell products—they sell immediacy. The language of "limited-time offer," "last chance," "only today" is not accidental; it is neuropsychologically engineered. Urgency marketing exploits what behavioural economists call *loss aversion*—our tendency to feel the pain of potential loss more acutely than the pleasure of equivalent gain. Scarcity, whether real or manufactured, triggers a primal response: act now or miss out. But in doing so, it replaces considered choice with conditioned response.

Social media compounds this effect by collapsing time and expanding comparison. Platforms once used to connect are now engines of curated performance, amplifying the visibility of others' success while muting their struggle. Every headline announcing a 25-year-old's startup exit, every viral reel showcasing a trading win or luxury purchase, silently whispers the same insinuation: *you are late.* The emotional pressure this creates is subtle but relentless. It suggests that wealth is not just about accumulation—it is about velocity. And if you're not moving quickly, you're not moving at all.

This is not a hypothetical concern. The psychological consequences are observable. Studies in behavioural finance have repeatedly shown that the average investor underperforms the markets not because they lack knowledge, but because they cannot sit still. They chase momentum, overreact to news, and panic in downturns—all behaviours exacerbated by platforms that treat volatility as spectacle. In a 2021 study conducted by Morningstar, investor returns consistently trailed fund returns due to mistimed entries and exits—a direct consequence of emotional interference driven by urgency. The implication is sobering: the more often people *act* under pressure, the worse they tend to perform.

Urgency also distorts career decisions. Professionals increasingly conflate speed of progress with quality of progress. The result is a generation of workers optimising for fast promotions, lateral jumps, and resume-building projects at the expense of mastery. But mastery, unlike mobility, compounds quietly. It demands repetition, patience, and periods of stagnation that today's hustle-centric culture finds intolerable. We are incentivised to appear busy, not to become good. The performance of productivity has, in many domains, replaced the reality of effectiveness.

There is also an ethical dimension to this problem. When urgency becomes the default tempo of decision-making, nuance is often the first casualty. Urgency is rarely a neutral force. It privileges speed over reflection, compression over complexity. It incentivises leaders to respond to headlines rather than long-term vision, to cut corners rather than build systems. This is especially dangerous in fields like investing, policy, and entrepreneurship—domains where long-term consequences are non-obvious and path dependencies are strong. An entrepreneur who pivots five times in a year may look agile, but they may also be lost. A fund manager who times the market aggressively may appear bold, but may also be gambling. The distinction is only visible through time—and urgency does not allow for time.

It would be a mistake, however, to attribute all blame to external systems. Urgency also satisfies something internal: the desire for control in a volatile world. Acting quickly *feels* like taking control. It provides the illusion of agency, even when the action is impulsive. This is why it persists. Slowing down, by contrast, demands comfort with ambiguity. It requires the ability to tolerate unknowing, to resist narrative closure, to sit with open-ended questions. These are not widely taught skills. In fact, they are increasingly countercultural.

There is a useful parallel here with the concept of *intertemporal choice* in behavioural economics—the decisions individuals make between immediate and delayed rewards. The famed Stanford marshmallow experiment is often cited to illustrate this, but newer research has gone deeper. Scholars have found that the ability to delay gratification is not just a moral trait, but a cognitive skill: it requires envisioning future states, projecting stability, and trusting in one's own strategy over external signals. In a world dominated by urgency, this ability is eroded. We are trained to distrust the future—to assume that unless action is taken *now*, all will be lost. This mental model is not only false, it is deeply counterproductive.

The financial industry has institutionalised urgency through design. Trading platforms celebrate activity. Notifications are framed in ways that trigger fear. "Market drop—should you adjust your portfolio?" "Tech stock surge—time to buy in?" These prompts are not informational; they are behavioural nudges. They do not ask you to think—they ask you to *react.* And reaction, in wealth-building, is almost always expensive. The most successful investors in history—from Warren Buffett to John Templeton—share a common trait: an extraordinary capacity to remain emotionally unmoved by urgency.

Their strength lies not in better information, but in *better emotional boundaries.*

Even outside of investing, this boundary becomes a strategic differentiator. In personal finance, urgency leads to lifestyle inflation. We are told that now is the time to upgrade, to purchase, to reward ourselves. Credit systems accommodate these desires, making future earnings vulnerable to present pressures. Marketing phrases such as "you deserve this now" masquerade as self-care but function as extraction tools. They shorten the time horizon of financial thinking, encouraging decisions that feel emotionally satisfying in the moment but structurally unstable in the long run.

But urgency's most insidious effect is epistemological: it changes how we define *value.* In a culture addicted to immediacy, long-term value is not just unseen—it is devalued. A decision that takes time to mature is seen as inefficient. A person who waits is seen as passive. A strategy that requires a quiet decade is seen as irrelevant. This distortion erodes not just wealth, but the very frameworks by which we evaluate what matters.

So what is the antidote? Certainly not slowness for its own sake. The counter to urgency is not inertia, but intentionality. It is the capacity to act not from pressure, but from principle. This requires recalibrating our relationship with time—not simply stretching it, but aligning it with purpose. It means choosing not based on immediacy, but based on strategic coherence. It means interrogating the sources of urgency in our lives and asking: *Who benefits when I move faster than I can think?*

This is not a call for retreat, but for discernment. It is a defence of the *pause*—the decision not to decide, the rare but powerful act of doing nothing when the world demands reaction. In markets, this manifests as holding through volatility. In careers, it looks like investing in skill rather than image. In personal finance, it means opting for sustainability over performance. And in life, it means building a philosophy that resists being dragged forward by every new signal, every new trend, every new fear.

Urgency is not the enemy of progress. But unexamined urgency is the enemy of wisdom. And in a world that rewards the illusion of speed, clarity itself becomes a competitive advantage. To reclaim that clarity requires an act of rebellion: to slow one's tempo, to expand one's horizon, and to remember that the most important decisions are rarely the ones that feel the most pressing. They are the ones that hold their value over time.

The Myth of Hustle Culture

Hustle culture is one of the most persistent—and perversely celebrated—myths in modern economic life. It dresses itself in the language of ambition and self-determination. It is popularised through punchy slogans, lauded in tech manifestos, and repackaged endlessly in the content mills of social media: *Wake up earlier. Sleep later. Outwork everyone. No days off.* On its surface, the narrative is seductive: anyone, from any background, can rise through sheer effort. Grind hard enough, and the system will eventually reward you. But behind this mythology lies a harsher reality—one in which endless work often leads not to sustainable wealth, but to burnout, poor decision-making, and a dangerously skewed relationship with time and value.

The appeal of hustle culture is not hard to understand. It promises control in a world that feels increasingly uncertain. In the context of volatile markets, stagnant wages, rising costs of living, and automation anxiety, hustle appears to offer an antidote to helplessness. It implies that outcomes are a direct function of effort—that the problem is not structural inequality or economic complexity, but personal laziness. This framing flatters the ego while obscuring inconvenient truths. It allows the system to remain unexamined because the blame, and the solution, rest entirely on the individual.

But effort alone is not a reliable predictor of long-term success. In many domains—particularly those involving capital markets, entrepreneurship, and creative work—*overactivity* often correlates with underperformance. Wealth-building, unlike manufacturing, does not scale linearly with input. It is a non-linear domain governed by timing, decision quality, and compounding. Excessive hustle, in this context, can lead to diminishing returns or outright self-sabotage. A trader glued to their screen may act too frequently and erode returns through fees and cognitive fatigue. An entrepreneur who pivots constantly may burn resources before product-market fit is ever achieved. A worker who sacrifices rest for output may find that chronic stress impairs the very cognition on which their future depends.

The deeper issue is that hustle culture glorifies motion over meaning. It incentivises visibility, not value. Metrics like "hours worked" or "projects started" become proxies for progress, even when they have little bearing on actual outcomes. In corporate settings, this often manifests as performative overwork: late-night emails, unnecessary meetings, and constant availability as a form of self-promotion. In the start-up world, it appears as the romanticisation of sleep deprivation, hustle porn, and the idea that success must be preceded by personal sacrifice to the point of collapse. But these behaviours do not necessarily indicate ambition—they often reflect anxiety and disorientation.

There is also a darker, more insidious cost: the erosion of discernment. When productivity becomes the sole currency of value, reflection is treated as waste. Strategic patience is reframed as stagnation. Saying "no" to a short-term opportunity in favour of long-term alignment is seen as a lack of drive. Over time, this distorts the individual's internal compass. The goal is no longer to build something meaningful or enduring, but simply to *keep moving*. And in this relentless movement, priorities blur. Financial plans become reactive. Investments are made hastily. Career decisions are guided by optics, not substance.

This is not a theoretical critique—it is observable in outcomes. Studies on worker wellbeing show a direct link between overwork and reduced cognitive function, impaired judgement, and increased rates of anxiety and depression. A 2019 meta-analysis published in *The Lancet* found that working more than 55 hours per week significantly increases the risk of stroke and heart disease. These are not minor trade-offs. They are evidence that the body and mind cannot be endlessly stretched in service of an ideology that mistakes exhaustion for excellence.

What is particularly troubling is how hustle culture exploits the very real desire to improve one's circumstances. In many cases, those who buy most deeply into the hustle narrative are those with the least margin for error—individuals from under-resourced backgrounds, first-generation professionals, and aspiring entrepreneurs without safety nets. The message they receive is clear: *You must outwork the system that wasn't built for you.* And while there is a kernel of truth in the idea that outsized effort is sometimes necessary, especially in early phases, the unspoken risk is that the system will absorb that effort without rewarding it—because effort, on its own, is not leverage.

Leverage is built through assets: skills, networks, intellectual property, equity ownership, and time. And the cultivation of these assets requires strategic focus, not constant grind. Warren Buffett did not build Berkshire Hathaway by working around the clock—he built it by waiting for the right bets and compounding his capital patiently. Patagonia's Yvon Chouinard spent much of his career climbing, surfing, and slowly growing a business aligned with his values. These individuals succeeded not through brute effort, but through *clear thinking*, aligned execution, and the emotional discipline to avoid unnecessary action. They were not less ambitious. They were more selective.

This contrast is important. Hustle culture suggests that the difference between success and failure is a matter of *volume*—more hours, more output, more hustle. But the difference is more often *friction.* Those who build sustainable wealth do so not by pushing harder, but by removing what impedes compounding. They say no often. They rest deliberately. They build systems that allow their time and capital to scale without constant intervention. Their work may be intense, but it is not frantic. It is laced with intentionality.

There is also a philosophical cost to the hustle mentality: it narrows the definition of a meaningful life. It implies that every moment not spent working is a moment wasted. That leisure must be earned through exhaustion. That identity is tethered exclusively to output. This view not only impoverishes the soul, it produces bad financial decisions. When rest is seen as indulgence rather than necessity, people burn out early and make reactive choices under cognitive strain. When status is defined by visible markers of hustle—luxury purchases, hyper-productivity, rapid growth—then people begin to optimise for *appearance* over *resilience.* And resilience, not image, is what sustains wealth across decades.

This distortion is particularly evident in the world of social media, where hustle culture finds its most enthusiastic audience. Influencers post time-stamped screenshots of 4 a.m. workouts, back-to-back meetings, and motivational quotes lifted from self-help mantras. The subtext is always the same: *If you're not doing this, you're not serious.* But this kind of performative ambition can be both deceptive and damaging. Many of these figures are monetising the illusion of success, not the substance. Their business is content, not enterprise. Their audience is being sold not a process, but a posture.

To break free from the myth of hustle culture is not to reject hard work—it is to reframe it. It is to understand that intensity is most valuable when it is intermittent and well-deployed, not constant and undirected. It is to recognise that *sustainability* is a more powerful filter for decisions than *maximum effort.* This applies equally to investing, entrepreneurship, and career planning. Wealth is rarely built by sprinting—it is built by positioning oneself well and staying solvent long enough for compounding to do its quiet work.

The future will increasingly reward those who can integrate rest with rigour, patience with planning, and clarity with constraint. Those who resist the pull of performative busyness and focus instead on *leverage*—on building durable skills, compounding relationships, and aligning effort with strategy—will be positioned not just to succeed, but to endure. That is the true measure of wealth. Not how hard one can grind, but how intelligently one can persist.

Hustle culture, at its most dangerous, teaches people to confuse activity with agency. It drowns out the deeper, slower work of reflection and alignment. It turns wealth-building into a theatre of motion, when in fact, the most valuable decisions are often the ones that take the most time—and the most restraint—to make. The myth must be replaced, not with passivity, but with a more honest model of ambition. One that rewards consistency over frenzy, discernment over desperation, and longevity over noise. Only then can we build lives—and portfolios—that are as rich in substance as they are in potential.

The Hidden Cost of Chasing Trends

Nothing destroys long-term wealth faster than short-term thinking dressed up as opportunity. One of the most underappreciated risks in personal finance today isn't ignorance—it's reactivity. The instinct to follow trends, to mimic the excitement of crowds, to capitalise on "once-in-a-lifetime" booms has repeatedly proven to be one of the most expensive habits a person can develop. Yet despite overwhelming evidence, this pattern persists. It thrives in market bubbles, it defines retail trading surges, and it is quietly embedded in the logic of speculative mania. It feels modern, urgent, and promising. But at its core, trend-chasing is an emotional reflex disguised as strategy—and the cost is not merely financial, but psychological and behavioural.

The psychology is deceptively simple. When we see others getting rich quickly, it creates emotional dissonance. We begin to doubt our patience, question our strategy, and recalibrate our sense of timing. We ask: *What if I'm missing out?* The fear of being left behind—socially, financially, or intellectually—can override even the most rational financial plans. This fear is ancient, rooted in evolutionary instincts. But in today's hyperconnected markets, it has been amplified to a level where behavioural contagion spreads faster than logic can intervene.

Consider the dot-com bubble of the late 1990s. The internet was transforming commerce, communication, and entire industries. The structural promise was real. But the valuations became decoupled from fundamentals. Companies with no revenue and no coherent business model received billion-dollar valuations simply for having ".com" in their names. Investors poured in, not because they understood the value proposition, but because others were pouring in. There was a collective suspension of critical judgment. When the bubble burst in 2000, trillions of dollars in market value vanished. Retirement portfolios were decimated. Start-ups evaporated overnight. And yet, the most instructive detail is not the collapse—

it is the fact that countless individuals ignored the warning signs because everyone else seemed confident.

We saw a mirror image of this pattern two decades later with the rise of meme stocks like GameStop and AMC. In early 2021, a coalition of retail investors, loosely coordinated through online forums like Reddit's WallStreetBets, launched a coordinated short squeeze that pushed these stocks to astronomical valuations. What began as a critique of institutional short-selling quickly transformed into a speculative frenzy. Day traders, inspired by viral posts and a sense of collective rebellion, jumped into trades they scarcely understood. Some made fortunes. Many more did not. The overwhelming majority who bought near the top—enticed by the visibility and emotional rush—suffered steep losses. The media focused on the drama; few headlines covered the quiet wreckage of individuals who mistook noise for knowledge.

This dynamic is not limited to equities. The cryptocurrency boom, particularly between 2017 and 2021, followed a similar script. Early adopters made generational wealth. But the broader retail wave was largely driven by speculation, not understanding. Coins with no utility or governance rigour soared purely on hype. Entire online cultures emerged around pumping certain tokens, with influencers offering "financial advice" based on price momentum rather than technological insight. The same FOMO dynamics applied. Those who entered late, often lacking an exit strategy or risk management framework, absorbed the downside of volatility without participating in the foundational upside. The volatility wasn't just market-based—it was emotional. And unlike capital, emotional resilience does not regenerate quickly.

The deeper issue is that trend-chasing distorts decision-making frameworks. It seduces people into timing markets rather than understanding them. It teaches that reward is proportional to urgency, rather than alignment. It encourages financial mimicry rather than independent judgment. Over time, this erodes an individual's ability to stick to a disciplined investment philosophy. Each bubble trains the brain to seek external cues rather than internal clarity. This is the real cost: not just lost capital, but lost sovereignty.

There is a cognitive cost as well. Reactive investing fatigues the mind. It places individuals in a constant state of vigilance, monitoring tickers, headlines, sentiment shifts. This attention depletion is not trivial. The human brain did not evolve for high-frequency, multi-signal environments. Decision fatigue sets in. Small errors compound. Anxiety rises. Eventually, even promising portfolios are abandoned—not because they were poorly designed, but because the investor became emotionally exhausted. Long-term wealth depends not only on financial return, but on the investor's ability to *remain invested.* Trend-chasing erodes that ability.

It is worth noting that not all trend-following is irrational. Some investors do specialise in momentum strategies or swing trading and possess the analytical infrastructure and temperament to execute them well. But this is a narrow segment of the market, not a model for the general investor. What's dangerous is when speculative behaviour becomes democratised without the corresponding tools, guardrails, or training. The marketing of trading apps as "gamified" platforms has played a major role in this trend. Interfaces designed to feel like casinos or social networks reduce friction to action. Buying options becomes as easy as ordering a meal. But the implications are far more enduring.

Part of what makes trend-chasing so difficult to resist is that it's usually rationalised after the fact. Individuals who lose money in speculative trades often reframe the experience as "learning." There is a place for this. But when losses are consistent, and the lessons unabsorbed, the cycle becomes pathological. Speculative behaviour becomes addictive. Like a gambler who believes the next hand will redeem the last, the investor seeks vindication rather than growth. In this context, wealth is not being built—it is being traded for fleeting emotional gratification.

To reverse this dynamic requires a conceptual shift. Wealth is not a story of bold moves. It is a story of durable positioning. Chasing trends places you on the outer edge of the cycle—buying when hype peaks, selling when fear dominates. This edge is volatile, emotionally taxing, and statistically unfavourable. Durable investors position themselves closer to the centre—where fundamentals guide action, timelines are longer, and emotional neutrality is prized. They are less visible in headlines, but far more consistent in outcomes.

Real-world data bears this out. DALBAR's annual studies have consistently shown that average investor returns fall well below the returns of the very funds they invest in, simply because of poor timing decisions. The performance gap is not about market structure—it is about behaviour. Investors buy after runs, sell during drawdowns, and repeat the pattern because they misinterpret what success looks like. In trend-driven investing, success is framed as beating the market. In reality, it should be framed as *staying in the market* long enough for quality decisions to compound.

There is an ethical dimension too, often ignored. Trend-chasing generates economic waste. It directs capital away from productive, long-term investments and into hype cycles that benefit few and leave many disillusioned. It creates perverse incentives for entrepreneurs to overstate, for media to sensationalise, and for regulators to play catch-up. When attention becomes the scarce resource, rather than capital, the quality of decision-making deteriorates across the board. Long-term innovation suffers when short-term speculation dominates.

A thoughtful investor, entrepreneur, or professional must therefore learn to distinguish signal from noise—and more critically, to resist conflating social validation with financial insight. A trend is not a thesis. Popularity is not predictive value. And timing, however tempting, is not a strategy—it is a gamble unless deeply embedded within a robust framework of risk, knowledge, and tolerance.

To build wealth that endures, the mind must be trained to disengage from reactive cycles. This does not mean ignoring trends entirely. It means interrogating them. Asking: *What problem does this solve? What value does it create? What price is already baked in? What is the exit plan?* More often than not, the trend fails under this scrutiny. And when it does, the decision not to participate becomes the most profitable action—because it preserves capital, energy, and focus for better opportunities.

The irony is that while trend-chasing feels like boldness, restraint requires more courage. To sit still while others sprint, to decline a seductive opportunity, to hold cash during a surge, or to stay invested during a correction—these are not passive decisions. They are *active expressions of emotional intelligence.* And they are, in the final analysis, the traits that distinguish those who merely trade from those who *outlast.*

The Time Horizon Deficit

The most overlooked variable in wealth creation is not income, access, or even intelligence—it is time. Not merely the passage of time, but *how* one perceives and relates to it. The human brain, when untrained, is naturally short-sighted. It reacts quickly, craves immediacy, and overweights the present at the expense of the future. In the modern financial landscape, this predisposition has been aggressively amplified. Today's investors and professionals operate within shrinking decision cycles, compressed expectations, and a culture of impatience that punishes delayed gratification. This phenomenon—a pervasive contraction of personal and institutional time horizons—is what we might accurately call the *time horizon deficit.* It is not just a cognitive error. It is a structural flaw in the way modern economies, markets, and individuals interpret risk, opportunity, and resilience.

To understand the cost of this deficit, consider how financial advice is increasingly framed. Market performance is reported hourly. Economic forecasts are revised weekly. Platforms encourage daily engagement. News outlets promote stock picks with 24-hour relevance. Even retirement planning, once a multi-decade exercise in disciplined saving, is now filtered through the lens of optimisation: how quickly can you "retire early," and what hacks will help you do so? The language has shifted from "long-term security" to "fast-track freedom." Under this logic, the goal is no longer to accumulate durable wealth through patience and discipline, but to win the game by compressing the timeline. This fundamentally distorts behaviour.

Markets, of course, reward time. Compound interest—the bedrock of investing—only functions when left undisturbed. Warren Buffett's fortune is not primarily a result of superior returns, but of *extraordinary duration*. He began investing in his teens and allowed compounding to work uninterrupted for over seventy years. Remove that time frame, and the numbers collapse. The same holds true for any meaningful financial strategy, from dollar-cost averaging to dividend reinvestment to real estate development. The returns are often nonlinear: negligible in the early years, exponential in later ones. A shortened horizon effectively severs this exponential tail. It leads people to exit too soon, panic too quickly, and chase strategies that promise immediacy at the expense of durability.

The contraction of time horizons is not limited to individuals. Corporations increasingly sacrifice long-term investment for short-term earnings visibility. Quarterly reporting cycles, pressure from activist shareholders, and performance-based executive compensation all contribute to this dynamic. The result is underinvestment in research, talent, and resilience-building systems—because those things do not pay off quickly. A McKinsey study of US companies found that those classified as "long-term oriented" significantly outperformed their short-term peers in revenue, earnings, and job creation over a fifteen-year window. But their approach requires weathering criticism, ambiguity, and deferred validation—all things that short-termism finds intolerable.

On an emotional level, shortened time horizons degrade resilience. When every fluctuation in a portfolio or project is interpreted as existential, anxiety increases and decision quality deteriorates. Emotional resilience is closely tied to temporal perspective. Individuals who can think in longer increments—five, ten, twenty years—are less reactive. They are more likely to endure volatility because they understand that most noise is self-correcting over time. By contrast, those trapped in short cycles are forced into hypervigilance. They make decisions under pressure, constantly seek new information, and are disproportionately influenced by the most recent events. This is not strategy. It is stress misinterpreted as analysis.

The irony is that the tools now available to the average investor are more powerful than ever. Access to global markets, data, automation, and diversification strategies has been democratised. Yet the average performance of individual investors remains poor, largely because their behaviour is governed by short-termism. They buy high, sell low, follow trends, and abandon plans prematurely. This is not a problem of access—it is a problem of time perception.

Part of the problem is that modern culture valorises speed. Startups are praised for their "velocity." Entrepreneurs are advised to "move fast and break things." Workers are incentivised to achieve results on compressed timelines, often at the expense of foundational competence. But long-term value creation is fundamentally incompatible with excessive speed. There is a natural cadence to mastery, market growth, and asset appreciation. Attempts to accelerate these processes tend to introduce risk, not efficiency.

Real estate offers a useful case study. Property markets, unlike equities, operate on longer cycles. They are less liquid, more locally influenced, and subject to structural constraints like zoning and development lag. Yet even here, time horizons are shrinking. Speculative flipping has replaced buy-and-hold investing in many markets. Investors aim for quick gains through leverage and timing rather than patient value creation. But this approach is highly vulnerable to macroeconomic shifts. Rising interest rates, regulatory changes, or demographic slowdowns can wipe out years of gains in a matter of months. The individuals most at risk are those who entered with a compressed timeline and no margin for error. They were not investors—they were *participants in a high-stakes timing exercise.*

To correct for the time horizon deficit, one must begin with conceptual clarity. What does it mean to think long-term? It does not mean ignoring present conditions or pretending volatility doesn't exist. It means integrating present decisions into a larger temporal framework. It means making choices that may not optimise the next six months, but significantly enhance the next six years. It involves a deliberate rejection of short-term validation in favour of long-term coherence. It is, in essence, a psychological shift—a transition from reacting to predicting, from chasing performance to constructing systems.

One of the most powerful illustrations of this principle comes from the world of pensions. Defined benefit pension funds, unlike most individual investors, operate on fifty-year time horizons. Their job is to match assets to liabilities decades in advance. As a result, they tend to allocate capital conservatively, diversify across geographies and asset classes, and avoid excessive turnover. Their performance, while rarely spectacular in the short run, tends to be remarkably stable over time. Contrast this with a high-frequency trader or a momentum investor, whose short-term returns may be explosive but whose strategies are highly sensitive to timing errors, liquidity constraints, and model drift. One relies on duration, the other on precision. In most cases, the former outlasts the latter.

What, then, are the practical consequences of this insight? At an individual level, it means structuring one's financial life around *systems* rather than *events*. A system might include automated saving, long-term asset allocation, periodic reviews, and the mental discipline to ignore daily market noise. Events, by contrast, are one-off decisions based on headlines, hunches, or sudden shifts in mood. Systems produce compounding results; events produce random outcomes. The former requires a time horizon aligned with your real goals—whether that is retirement, intergenerational wealth transfer, or creative independence.

The same logic applies outside finance. Careers built on short-term optimisation—job hopping, salary maximisation, brand chasing—often plateau sooner than those built on depth, relationships, and skill stacking. Relationships governed by immediacy tend to be more fragile than those cultivated through consistency. Even health outcomes are time-sensitive: the benefits of exercise, sleep, and nutrition accumulate slowly but decisively. In nearly every domain that matters, time is the invisible multiplier of effort.

This is not to say that agility or adaptation are unimportant. Flexibility within a long-term frame is crucial. But flexibility without a frame is chaos. One must know the difference between iteration and distraction. Between a short-term pivot that strengthens long-term strategy and one that replaces it. This discernment is only possible when a clear time horizon has been established—and committed to emotionally.

Ultimately, the time horizon deficit is not a data problem. It is not solved through better information or sharper predictions. It is a discipline problem—a failure to think, act, and feel in sync with what enduring outcomes actually require. Wealth, real wealth, is not built by predicting the next quarter. It is built by *living in alignment with the next decade.* And the further you can stretch your mental time horizon—without losing sight of practical execution—the greater your emotional resilience, your decision clarity, and your probability of building something that lasts.

Chapter 2
The Biology of Impatience: Your Brain on Risk and Reward

Most financial missteps do not originate in spreadsheets; they arise in the mind. Behind every rash trade, every hurried sell-off, every purchase that later brings regret lies a nervous system designed for survival, not for compounding wealth. The human brain—honed over hundreds of millennia—was built to spot threats, secure resources, and seize rewards while they were available. It was not designed to weigh distant risks, wait calmly for delayed outcomes, or sit through turbulence without reacting. This mismatch between ancient biology and modern finance is more than an intellectual curiosity; it is the root of countless errors. It explains why patience is scarce in practice, why so many investors underperform their own portfolios, and why emotional discipline, though endlessly praised, is so rare. To grasp how fortunes endure—or unravel—we must begin with this: the biology of impatience.

The starting insight is disarmingly simple: your brain is not on your side when it comes to patience. It never has been. Patience is not a natural setting; it is a hard-won override. Our ancestors lived with scarcity as the default, where hesitation could cost survival. Resources were consumed when found, decisions made under pressure, short-term thinking rewarded. The circuitry that drove this behaviour endures, encoded in the dopamine system. Often mislabelled the "pleasure chemical," dopamine is in fact the neurotransmitter of anticipation. It does not surge when we receive a reward, but when we expect one. The stronger the anticipation, the more urgent the impulse to act—and to act immediately.

From this emerges what might be called the dopamine economy, a culture organised around stimulating the urge to act, not the discipline to wait. Markets and media, apps and algorithms—all lean into this circuitry. Flashing updates, news alerts, likes and notifications: these are triggers designed to provoke dopamine spikes. Checking an investment app multiple times a day is rarely about information; it is the brain seeking novelty, reassurance, or excitement. The result is not rational monitoring but a feedback loop akin to addiction. And like all addictions, it shrinks horizons, dulls judgement, and corrodes long-term aims.

Yet reward is only half the story. The other half is fear, rooted in the amygdala—a small almond-shaped structure whose job is threat detection. When risk is sensed, especially in uncertain environments, the amygdala fires quickly and disproportionately. On the savannah, that hair-trigger response saved lives. In markets, it wreaks havoc. The threats of finance are abstract and statistical. But the amygdala does not parse abstraction; it reacts as though danger were immediate. A ten per cent drop on a balance sheet is read as catastrophe, prompting flight responses—sell now, escape while you can. Thus panic selling, chronic anxiety, and the underestimation of recovery potential.

Seen this way, what passes as poor financial judgement is often untrained neurobiology. The machinery itself is sound, but it is operating in the wrong environment. A market correction registers as mortal danger. A missed gain threatens identity. A deferred return feels like punishment. Illogical, perhaps—but biologically coherent. Unless retrained, the brain continues to misfire in the same ways: chasing too soon, fleeing too early, undermining the very patience on which wealth depends.

Consider the famous Marshmallow Test of the 1960s. Children were offered one marshmallow immediately or two if they could wait fifteen minutes. Those who waited tended, decades later, to show stronger life outcomes—academically, relationally, financially. The experiment became a parable of delayed gratification. Yet later research revealed a more layered truth: waiting was not merely about willpower. It depended on environment—whether the child trusted the adult's promise, whether previous needs had been reliably met, whether delay had ever yielded reward. Translated into financial life, the lesson is stark. Patience rests on trust: in systems, in institutions, in one's future self. To cultivate patience, then, is to build environments where waiting is rational—where time pays.

Here enters neuroplasticity, the brain's ability to rewire through experience. It provides a counter-narrative to biological determinism. The brain is not fixed; emotional steadiness can be trained like a muscle. This possibility changes everything. Investors, entrepreneurs, decision-makers can cultivate the ability to withstand uncertainty, reinterpret volatility, and lengthen horizons. It requires deliberate practice—reflection, routines that temper reactivity, exposure to evidence that challenges bias. But it is possible. A mind that once panicked at every downturn can learn to see opportunity. A brain once restless for stimulation can learn to sit quietly. This is not emotional suppression. It is cognitive retraining—teaching the mind to interpret its own signals with greater subtlety.

What we confront here is not simply quirks of psychology but the operating system itself. Every system has defaults, limitations, and upgrade paths. If your wealth strategy assumes pure rationality, it is doomed. Not because reason is irrelevant, but because it is too slow. Deeper circuits fire first. You cannot out-think the amygdala in the moment; you must anticipate it. Build buffers: rules, automatic safeguards, social constraints. Design not for the brain you admire in theory, but for the one you actually carry.

This chapter will unpick these elements in turn. We will begin with dopamine—how it drives action, how modern systems exploit it, and how to manage it without rejecting reward altogether. We will examine the mechanics of fear, showing how the amygdala hijacks reason when scarcity is perceived. We will revisit delayed gratification, moving past the simplistic morality tale to see the environmental and neurological conditions that make patience possible. Finally, we will turn to neuroplasticity, exploring how the brain can be trained to tolerate uncertainty, extend horizons, and moderate volatility.

The aim is not simply to explain why people act rashly with money. It is to show what can be done about it. Impatience is not a pathology; it is a legacy. To overcome it requires understanding its roots and then building systems robust enough to contain it. This is not a plea for superhuman composure. It is an argument for consciousness: the recognition that wealth over time is less about perfect timing or privileged access, and more about emotional regulation. And regulation begins not in abstract theories, but in the neural machinery we inherit and can, with effort, reshape.

You are not irrational because you panic. You panic because your brain is designed to. But what you construct with that brain—how you train it, how you defend it against its own impulses—will decide whether you become prey to the cycles of speculation or the deliberate architect of your own financial resilience. The blueprint already exists within you. The task is to read it carefully, and begin the building.

The Dopamine Economy

The average person today receives more stimuli in a single hour than their ancestors encountered in days. Alerts ping, portfolios update, feeds refresh, opportunities surface and vanish with the flick of a finger. Underneath all this activity is not just technology or choice—it is chemistry. Specifically, the brain's reward system, driven in large part by dopamine. The modern economy is not simply one of supply and demand—it is a dopamine economy, calibrated not to long-term value, but to short-term neurological satisfaction. This presents a fundamental problem for wealth creation, because the system that now governs attention, decision-making, and motivation is optimised for *impulse*, not patience. Understanding how dopamine governs behaviour is no longer optional for investors, professionals, or consumers—it is essential.

Dopamine, often mislabelled as the brain's "pleasure molecule," is more accurately described as the *anticipation neurotransmitter*. It is not about enjoyment itself, but about *what might happen next*. It fuels pursuit. When dopamine levels rise, we are drawn toward novelty, reward cues, and perceived gains. This is evolutionarily useful. In hunter-gatherer societies, it motivated individuals to explore new territories, seek food, and pursue potential mates. But in modern financial contexts, this same circuitry leads people to chase short-term rewards—stock tips, crypto pumps, gamified apps—without regard for long-term outcomes. The problem is not dopamine per se, but the mismatch between an ancient motivational system and a contemporary environment engineered to exploit it.

Today's financial technologies are built with this biology in mind. Brokerages, trading apps, and digital wallets increasingly mimic the design language of social media platforms. Bright colours, rapid feedback, push notifications, and performance badges activate the same reward systems as video games or Instagram likes. The result is not financial engagement, but *dopaminergic engagement*—users are not drawn to strategy or substance, but to stimulation. Behavioural economists have documented that the more frequently users check their investment apps, the worse their long-term returns tend to be. This is not irrational behaviour—it is chemically reinforced behaviour. People are acting on a script that predates modern finance by millennia.

This script makes it harder to stay still. When the brain is flooded with anticipatory dopamine, waiting feels like failure. Patience becomes indistinguishable from boredom, and inactivity feels emotionally uncomfortable. This has profound implications for investing. Compounding—the single most powerful force in wealth creation—requires long periods of doing *nothing*. It demands emotional neutrality, time insulation, and a tolerance for slow progress. But in a dopamine-saturated system, slow progress registers as *no progress*. Investors become vulnerable to action bias: the impulse to do *something*—anything—because stillness feels like a missed opportunity. The long-term strategy is abandoned for short-term sensation.

Consider the behavioural profile of the average retail investor during speculative surges. When meme stocks like GameStop or AMC went parabolic in 2021, millions of new investors were swept into the fray. The promise was not simply financial return—it was narrative return: excitement, identity, rebellion. These are powerful dopamine cues. Online communities offered rapid feedback loops, social reinforcement, and a sense of urgency. For many participants, the dopamine spike of *belonging* and *anticipating gain* outweighed the rational evaluation of risk. Some profited. Most did not. But across the board, behaviour was driven more by *emotionally charged pursuit* than by financially grounded planning.

What makes dopamine especially insidious in financial settings is that it creates a loop. The more often a behaviour is rewarded, even intermittently, the stronger the loop becomes. This is called variable reinforcement—a pattern known to create powerful compulsions in gambling environments. You don't need to win every time to become hooked. You just need to win *occasionally*, and unexpectedly. Day trading platforms have adopted this model, whether consciously or not. Users who experience occasional spikes in portfolio value are more likely to return, increase frequency, and escalate risk. Over time, decision-making becomes less about strategy and more about *chasing the high*. This is not a metaphor—it is a literal neurological process.

Importantly, dopamine is not always the villain. It is essential for motivation, learning, and exploration. The problem arises when it dominates cognition to the exclusion of other regulatory mechanisms. In a healthy financial decision-making model, dopamine is balanced by prefrontal activity—executive functions like planning, reflection, and inhibition. This balance allows individuals to weigh short-term incentives against long-term consequences. But the more dopamine is activated—especially in environments of uncertainty and novelty—the harder it is for prefrontal systems to maintain control. The result is an internal imbalance that favours impulsive, often suboptimal choices.

There is evidence to suggest that this imbalance can be exacerbated by sleep deprivation, stress, and information overload—conditions that are, not coincidentally, endemic to high-paced financial culture. Chronic exposure to market news, social media feeds, and economic volatility places the brain in a semi-permanent state of alertness. Dopamine levels remain elevated, prefrontal resources are depleted, and the ability to make calm, strategic decisions deteriorates. What begins as engagement becomes addiction. What begins as informed vigilance becomes reactive obsession.

The solution is not to demonise dopamine, but to manage its influence intentionally. This begins with environment design. Just as architects use physical space to shape behaviour, financial environments can be structured to reduce impulsive triggers. This might include limiting exposure to real-time price updates, disabling push notifications, or using software that enforces investment horizons. Some sophisticated investors automate their decisions entirely, removing themselves from emotionally charged contexts. They understand that their *system* is a better decision-maker than their *state*.

Another critical intervention is awareness. Understanding the dopamine cycle—anticipation, action, reward—enables individuals to pause and interrogate their impulses. "Why do I feel the need to act now? Is this based on strategy or stimulation?" These are not abstract reflections; they are tools for regaining control of cognitive agency. Financial education that includes *neurobiological literacy* is far more powerful than education based solely on rules or historical data. People do not lose money because they lack information. They lose money because they lack mechanisms to *resist* information that hijacks their attention.

It is also worth noting that the financial industry has a vested interest in keeping dopamine high. Transaction-based platforms, content creators, and short-term funds benefit when people act more frequently. This creates a perverse incentive structure in which the emotional state most harmful to individual wealth is the one most profitable to institutions. Dopamine is not just a neurotransmitter—it is an economic driver. Its manipulation is baked into the architecture of modern finance, and those who fail to see this are at a structural disadvantage.

To thrive in this environment, one must become what behavioural scientists call a "meta-cognitive investor"—someone who not only evaluates external variables, but actively monitors internal states. They know when their dopamine is firing, when their fear is rising, and when their patience is thinning. They do not trust their instincts blindly. They build systems that compensate for those instincts. They understand that enduring wealth is not about being right more often, but about being *reactive less often.* They protect their focus as diligently as they protect their capital—because they understand that in a dopamine economy, attention is the first asset to be extracted.

This subchapter is not an argument against innovation, speed, or technology. It is an argument for *neurological sovereignty*—for regaining control over the systems that increasingly shape our decisions. In the chapters that follow, we will examine the fear response, delayed gratification, and the science of neuroplasticity. But dopamine is the starting point. It explains why we move before we think, why we chase what we don't need, and why we so often sabotage the very strategies we claim to follow. The future of financial resilience will not belong to those who know the most—but to those who can remain composed when their brains are screaming for action. That begins by understanding the chemistry of the scream.

The Threat Response Hijack

In moments of crisis, your rationality is rarely the first system to arrive. Long before analysis, long before risk-reward calculations, and long before coherent thoughts can form, another part of the brain has already taken control. That part is the amygdala—a primitive but powerful structure deep in the limbic system, responsible for detecting threats and triggering survival responses. Its activation is fast, automatic, and largely unconscious. This mechanism kept our ancestors alive in the wild. But in modern financial contexts—volatile markets, economic uncertainty, and investment drawdowns—it can be catastrophically misapplied. The same system that once helped you evade a predator is now prompting you to sell your holdings in a short-term panic. It's not simply a bad decision. It's a *neurobiological hijack*.

The amygdala operates on speed, not subtlety. When faced with uncertainty or threat, it activates a cascade of physiological changes: adrenaline surges, heart rate increases, attention narrows, and complex reasoning is suppressed in favour of immediate action. This "fight or flight" response is not optional—it is hardwired. In a financial context, this translates into a disproportionate fear of loss, a hyper-focus on worst-case scenarios, and an urgency to act *now* in order to avoid perceived danger. But modern financial threats are not immediate or mortal. They are probabilistic, abstract, and long-horizon. The amygdala does not understand this. It interprets a 15% market dip as an existential threat and urges total exit. It cannot distinguish between *temporary volatility* and *permanent loss*. This distinction must be imposed by the rational mind—if it has not already been overridden.

This override is surprisingly common. Neuroimaging studies show that during periods of financial stress—such as market crashes or portfolio losses—the amygdala lights up with activity similar to that seen in life-threatening scenarios. The result is not just fear, but impaired cognition. The prefrontal cortex, responsible for deliberation and long-term planning, effectively goes offline. In this state, investors make decisions they would never endorse under calmer conditions: panic selling during a correction, abandoning a well-researched strategy, moving entirely to cash at the bottom of a cycle. These decisions feel rational in the moment because the threat feels real. But they are driven by biology, not strategy.

The 2008 global financial crisis offers a sobering example. During the steepest market declines, many individual investors liquidated their portfolios in a state of fear. Those who sold in late 2008 or early 2009 locked in substantial losses, missing the powerful recovery that followed. By 2013, markets had not only recovered but reached new highs—yet many who had exited early remained underinvested for years, traumatised by the experience. This was not simply a failure of information. It was a failure of *emotional regulation under threat.* The amygdala had hijacked their financial agency, and the cost was measured in years of lost compounding.

This hijack extends beyond panic selling. It also fuels risk aversion in ways that quietly erode long-term returns. Investors who experience a market downturn early in their financial life often develop a persistent underallocation to equities, even when fundamentals would justify a more growth-oriented stance. The amygdala remembers. It encodes fear far more strongly than reward. This asymmetry leads to cautious behaviour that feels safe but may be economically suboptimal. Over decades, this can significantly depress wealth accumulation—not through dramatic losses, but through *chronically missed opportunities.*

Fear also distorts the perception of randomness. When the brain is in a threat response, it looks for patterns, causes, and intentions—even where none exist. This creates a cognitive vulnerability to conspiracy theories, magical thinking, and the allure of protective narratives. It is no coincidence that doomsday predictions gain traction during bear markets. The emotional state created by falling prices predisposes the mind to believe that *something is fundamentally broken.* This belief feels safer than accepting uncertainty. It provides psychological closure at the cost of analytical accuracy.

The challenge, then, is not simply to suppress fear—it is to *manage its influence.* This begins with understanding the latency mismatch between the amygdala and the rational mind. The amygdala responds in milliseconds. Rational analysis takes seconds or minutes. In between, there is a window of vulnerability during which impulsive actions can be initiated. Preventing destructive decisions requires creating systems that operate faster than fear. This might include automatic investment plans, pre-set rebalancing rules, or predetermined thresholds for review—not reaction. These structures act as buffers, allowing the emotional wave to pass before action is taken.

Experienced investors often do this intuitively. They develop rituals, checklists, and behavioural constraints that reduce the likelihood of amygdala-led decisions. They may take walks before trading, discuss concerns with a peer before acting, or maintain written investment theses that anchor their thinking during periods of volatility. These practices are not signs of weakness—they are signs of *strategic humility*. They acknowledge that fear is inevitable and that no amount of intelligence will prevent its initial surge. But they also demonstrate that intelligent systems can be built to contain it.

There is also an ethical implication here that should not be ignored. The financial industry—and the media that feeds it—often profits from activating the threat response. Sensationalist headlines, click-driven content, and fear-based marketing all exploit amygdala sensitivity. "Markets in turmoil," "Is your portfolio at risk?" "Experts warn of impending crash"—these phrases are not neutral. They are triggers. They generate engagement precisely because they activate the emotional systems most likely to override careful thought. This is not an information problem; it is a manipulation problem. Recognising this dynamic is not about paranoia. It is about reclaiming agency.

To resist the threat response hijack, one must cultivate both structural discipline and emotional awareness. Structural discipline involves the design of environments and systems that reduce the opportunity for impulsive action. Emotional awareness involves recognising the physiological and psychological signs of fear—tight chest, racing thoughts, compulsive checking—and treating them as signals to *pause*, not to act. Both capacities can be trained. Neuroplasticity ensures that the brain can learn new patterns of response. Over time, the neural pathways associated with fear-based action can be weakened, and those associated with calm evaluation can be strengthened. But this process is neither automatic nor fast. It requires repetition, reflection, and a deliberate engagement with discomfort.

It also requires reframing what volatility means. Volatility is not a threat. It is a condition of markets—a natural byproduct of decentralised information processing. The amygdala interprets it as danger because it resembles chaos. But a sophisticated investor sees volatility as a pricing mechanism, a source of opportunity, and sometimes even a protective feature. Assets with zero volatility often offer zero return. Volatility is not what harms investors—*the response to it is.*

Understanding the threat response hijack reframes the challenge of investing. It is not simply about finding the right assets or the best strategy. It is about learning to *outlast your own nervous system.* To do this well is to build wealth not just in monetary terms, but in emotional resilience, cognitive clarity, and behavioural consistency. In markets, as in life, those who can remain stable when others are reactive gain a decisive advantage—not by being fearless, but by being prepared. And preparation, in this context, begins not with charts or forecasts, but with the amygdala—and the systems we build to keep it in check.

The Delayed Gratification Paradox

Patience is often praised as a virtue, but in the context of human cognition, it is far from natural. The default setting of the brain is not to wait. It is to act, to consume, to secure resources in the present—because for most of our evolutionary history, the present was all we could trust. Delayed gratification, then, is not a spontaneous trait. It is a cognitive achievement, one that sits atop a fragile scaffolding of trust, security, and learned regulation. Nowhere is this paradox more vividly illustrated than in the Marshmallow Test, a behavioural study that captured the public imagination but is widely misunderstood in both its findings and implications.

In the original Stanford experiment led by psychologist Walter Mischel in the late 1960s, young children were offered a simple choice: eat one marshmallow now, or wait 15 minutes and receive two. The test was elegant, intuitive, and yielded a compelling narrative. Follow-up studies suggested that those who could wait—those who delayed gratification—went on to score higher on standardised tests, attain higher levels of education, and exhibit better emotional regulation in adulthood. The implication was clear: self-control in early childhood predicted life success. The Marshmallow Test became shorthand for character strength, the educational system embraced it as evidence for social-emotional learning, and pop psychology turned it into a litmus test for future prosperity.

But the reality was more complicated. Later studies, including a 2018 replication with a larger and more diverse sample, revealed that the relationship between delayed gratification and life outcomes was not nearly as strong once socioeconomic variables were controlled. In other words, children who came from more stable, resource-rich environments were more likely to wait—not because they had more willpower, but because *waiting made sense.* They had reason to believe that the second marshmallow would still be there. This insight reframes the test entirely. It was never a pure measure of self-control. It was a test of *environmental trust* and *strategic inference.*

This matters because it challenges the assumption that impatience is a moral weakness. In reality, it may be an adaptation to unpredictability. If your lived experience has taught you that resources are scarce, that promises are not always kept, or that good things are routinely taken away, then acting now is not impulsive—it is rational. This reframing has profound implications for how we understand financial behaviour. Many individuals who make short-term decisions—whether spending instead of saving, cashing out investments prematurely, or chasing immediate returns—are not failing at logic. They are enacting a logic that has been shaped by their personal history, environment, and perception of risk.

The delayed gratification paradox, then, is this: we assume that waiting is universally better, but *the willingness to wait depends on the belief that the wait will be rewarded.* Without that belief, even intelligent individuals will opt for immediacy. This is not a failure of values—it is a failure of expected value. And expected value is deeply contextual.

Modern finance exacerbates this tension. It demands long time horizons, disciplined contributions, and tolerance for volatility—yet it bombards individuals with real-time signals that contradict this ethic. Newsfeeds, trading platforms, and social media reward immediacy with feedback, affirmation, and dopamine. They incentivise action, not restraint. In this environment, delayed gratification is not merely difficult—it is counter-cultural. Individuals are constantly being nudged to prioritise the now: to take the bonus, book the gains, buy the lifestyle, maximise the quarter. Patience feels like inaction. Inaction feels like failure.

Yet the data is unequivocal: across nearly every domain of wealth-building, the most successful strategies are those that defer gratification. Long-term investment strategies outperform reactive ones. Career paths built on depth, rather than lateral movement, yield greater autonomy and earnings over time. Businesses that reinvest in quality and culture compound their advantage. But these outcomes require individuals to sit with uncertainty, forgo short-term validation, and tolerate the absence of immediate feedback. In a world optimised for distraction, that is no small task.

So how do we reconcile this biological and environmental mismatch? The answer lies not in preaching patience, but in *training it.* If delayed gratification is a skill, not a trait, then it can be developed—through intentional design, feedback loops, and small, repeated acts of self-regulation. One promising approach is "commitment devices": structures that limit access to impulsive actions. Automatic savings plans, for instance, remove the temptation to spend by separating the decision from the moment of reward. Investment platforms that restrict daily trading, or that delay fund transfers, use friction to protect long-term goals. These are not constraints—they are safeguards against the impulsive logic of the untrained brain.

Another approach is to cultivate what behavioural scientists call *episodic future thinking*—the ability to vividly imagine a future self and attribute value to their outcomes. When individuals are asked to visualise themselves in retirement, or to write letters to their future selves, they are more likely to make decisions aligned with long-term interests. This is because the brain treats abstract future states as less "real" unless made concrete. Bridging this temporal gap reduces the emotional discounting of future rewards—a core challenge in behavioural finance.

Education also plays a central role, but not in the form most people expect. Financial literacy is helpful, but insufficient. What's needed is *emotional literacy*: the ability to recognise the feelings that drive short-termism, to name them, and to build reflective pauses into decision-making. A person who knows the math behind compounding but panics at the first market dip has knowledge without resilience. A person who understands volatility in theory but interprets every loss as failure will not stay the course. Teaching people how to *feel* through uncertainty may be more important than teaching them how to model returns.

There is also a collective dimension to this problem. Individual patience is often undermined by systemic short-termism. Employers that reward quarterly results, governments that operate on electoral cycles, and institutions that benchmark performance in real time all send the message that long-term thinking is for idealists, not professionals. This creates a cultural drag on delayed gratification, one that can't be offset by personal discipline alone. If society wants to nurture patience, it must stop punishing it.

Still, there is room for optimism. Neuroscience shows that the brain is plastic, even into adulthood. New circuits can be formed. Old habits can be rewired. And small, repeated acts of restraint can lead to larger behavioural shifts over time. A person who consistently defers minor purchases builds the neural pathways that allow them to delay larger ones. A professional who practises strategic silence in meetings becomes better at withstanding the need to fill every gap with activity. A parent who models thoughtful delay teaches their children that waiting is not passive—it is powerful.

This perspective reframes delayed gratification not as a rigid virtue but as a *flexible competence*. It is not a test you pass in childhood, but a capacity you build across contexts. It can be eroded by fear, but also reinforced by structure. It is not a fixed identity—it is a dynamic interplay between biology, environment, and belief. And perhaps most importantly, it is not merely about saying "no" to the present. It is about saying "yes" to a future that feels *real enough* to matter.

To build wealth—true, enduring wealth—requires not just knowledge, but *temporal imagination.* It requires individuals to anchor decisions in futures they cannot yet touch, to trust processes that do not offer daily validation, and to practise a form of maturity that modern systems neither demand nor reward. That is the paradox. And that is the path forward.

Neuroplasticity and Emotional Mastery

The most transformative insight in modern neuroscience is not about intelligence, memory, or genetics. It is about change. The brain, once thought to be fixed after childhood, is in fact *plastic*—capable of rewiring itself structurally and functionally throughout life. This capacity, known as neuroplasticity, offers more than academic fascination. It offers practical hope. It tells us that even our most ingrained behavioural patterns—impulsivity, anxiety under uncertainty, aversion to patience—are not hard limits. They are neural habits, formed through repetition, and they can be reshaped. For those seeking to build lasting wealth in a world saturated with volatility and noise, this is not just a psychological advantage. It is a strategic imperative.

Patience is not a character trait you either possess or lack. It is a neural pathway reinforced by experience. Tolerance for ambiguity is not a rare gift; it is a skill that can be trained through structured exposure. Emotional mastery, in this context, is not about suppressing feelings. It is about *changing the brain's relationship to discomfort.* This reframing is vital because many people mistakenly approach emotional resilience as a fixed personality variable, rather than as a set of capacities that can be developed through conscious effort and designed environments. Neuroplasticity is the science that validates this view—and opens the door to practical intervention.

The neural mechanisms of plasticity are now well understood. Repeated activation of a particular circuit—be it physical, cognitive, or emotional—strengthens the synaptic connections involved. Neurons that fire together, wire together. This means that every time we respond to uncertainty with calm rather than panic, every time we pause before acting on impulse, every time we choose to wait rather than react, we are literally altering the structure of our brain. These changes are not metaphorical. They are measurable in functional imaging studies and observable in behavioural outcomes. In high-performing individuals—from long-term investors to elite athletes to seasoned negotiators—patterns of calm reactivity are not simply preferred; they are *embedded.* They have been practised to the point of automation.

Yet the environment plays an equally critical role. Neuroplasticity is not a blank cheque. The brain changes in response to input, and if the dominant input is reactive, fear-based, and fragmented, the neural outcome will reflect that. This is why emotional mastery is so rare in digital finance cultures. Platforms that reward immediacy, interrupt concentration, and amplify volatility are actively training the opposite of patience. They are conditioning users into short feedback loops, high-salience cues, and rapid-fire response patterns. Over time, this erodes the brain's capacity for extended focus and measured judgement. Neuroplasticity cuts both ways.

To counteract this drift, one must build deliberate training protocols—habits and practices that slowly recondition the brain to value stability over stimulation. Meditation, for instance, is not a wellness cliché. It is a proven method of strengthening the prefrontal cortex while reducing amygdala activity. Studies show that long-term meditators exhibit increased cortical thickness in regions associated with attention, emotional regulation, and self-awareness. These are the same regions implicated in high-quality financial decision-making. Likewise, structured exposure to uncertainty—through controlled risk-taking or volatility tolerance exercises—can recalibrate the brain's threat response. When individuals learn, repeatedly, that discomfort is not danger, they begin to uncouple the sensation of anxiety from the necessity of reaction.

This is particularly relevant in investment contexts. Investors who check their portfolios daily are not simply uninformed—they are conditioning themselves into myopic loss aversion. Each dip, each spike, each anomalous event becomes encoded as meaningful. But from a neuroplastic perspective, this reinforces hypervigilance and shortens the emotional time horizon. The investor becomes neurologically primed to react, even when rational analysis would advise stillness. By contrast, investors who train themselves to ignore noise—who review performance quarterly, automate contributions, and focus on process rather than outcome—develop a different neurological profile. Their brains are not immune to volatility, but they are less governed by it.

Real-world case studies reinforce this. Consider the behavioural difference between two equally intelligent investors: one who checks the market every morning, reads financial news obsessively, and reacts to each movement with tension; and another who has a clear strategy, limits information intake, and views downturns as normal conditions. Over a decade, the difference in returns may be less pronounced than the difference in stress, consistency, and emotional attrition. The second investor is not simply more disciplined—they are *better wired.* Their behaviour flows not from exceptional willpower, but from a brain that has been shaped by years of making high-quality decisions under conditions of ambiguity.

Neuroplasticity also provides a critical counterweight to deterministic thinking. Many people assume that because they have historically struggled with anxiety, reactivity, or short-termism, they are simply "not wired" for investing or strategic thinking. But this is a misunderstanding of how plasticity works. The very fact that these patterns exist *proves* that the brain is malleable. They were learned—usually unconsciously, through repeated exposure and reinforcement—and they can be unlearned. This is not motivational rhetoric. It is the core finding of hundreds of studies in behavioural neuroscience and cognitive therapy.

Crucially, emotional mastery through neuroplasticity does not mean emotional suppression. The goal is not to become detached or indifferent. Emotions carry information. Fear can highlight risk. Excitement can signal opportunity. But when these emotions are experienced without *agency*—when they trigger automatic behaviours rather than informed decisions—they become liabilities. Emotional mastery is about maintaining access to your higher-order thinking *while* feeling what you feel. It is about slowing the loop between stimulus and response so that intention can enter.

To facilitate this, a number of practical techniques are supported by the science. One is *reframing*—the practice of consciously interpreting ambiguous situations in a way that supports long-term objectives. A market drop, rather than being seen as a threat, is framed as a discount. A delayed reward is framed not as deprivation, but as *accrued value*. This is not just semantics. fMRI studies show that reframing activates different neural circuits than passive emotional response. Over time, these circuits can become default pathways, reducing the intensity of threat perception and increasing tolerance for ambiguity.

Another technique is *graded exposure*. Just as athletes build tolerance through progressive overload, individuals can build emotional tolerance by gradually increasing their exposure to discomfort in controlled ways. For example, an investor might begin by observing market volatility without acting, then by extending the interval between decision points, then by practising inaction during moderate corrections. Each step builds both confidence and neural adaptation. What felt intolerable becomes manageable—not because the market has changed, but because the brain has.

It is also essential to normalise setbacks. Neuroplastic change is non-linear. There will be regressions, days when fear takes over, moments of impatience. The mistake is to interpret these as proof of failure. In fact, they are evidence of the system at work. Each return to equilibrium after a disruption strengthens the new pattern. Each resisted impulse reinforces the pathway of restraint. Mastery is not the absence of impulse. It is the capacity to notice it, pause, and choose.

Ultimately, neuroplasticity offers a powerful narrative shift. You are not at the mercy of your instincts, your history, or even your temperament. You are operating a system that adapts to input. And if you understand that system—if you respect its constraints while exploiting its malleability—you can design a mind that serves your strategy rather than sabotaging it. Emotional patience is not gifted. It is *grown.* And like any compounding asset, it rewards consistency far more than intensity. In a world where everyone is chasing advantage through information, speed, or access, the quiet power of rewiring your own brain may be the most underappreciated edge of all.

Chapter 3
The Philosophy of Endurance: Timeless Wisdom for Modern Wealth

Wealth, in the way it is most often imagined today, is spoken of almost exclusively in the vocabulary of movement—strategies and side-hustles, optimisations, accelerators, clever tricks. The dominant culture praises urgency above composure, doing over waiting, strain over restraint. What slips from notice—because it resists packaging, selling, or broadcasting—is the quieter scaffolding beneath lasting wealth: endurance. Not the dramatic, cinematic version of endurance, but the ordinary kind—measured restraint, patient stillness, disciplined refusal to overreact. In a civilisation addicted to immediacy, endurance feels almost subversive. Yet it is this quality, more than brilliance or luck, that governs whether wealth is preserved, not merely acquired.

Here, endurance is treated not as a quirk of personality but as a deliberate philosophy—a way of seeing and acting that braids together resilience, lucidity, and moral weight. Unlike passive patience, endurance is active governance of the self. It poses sharper questions: not just whether we can wait, but whether we can wait wisely. Whether coherence can be maintained under strain. Whether we can resist mistaking movement for progress. Endurance, properly understood, is a practice—a cultivated discipline grounded in centuries of reflection. And its relevance to wealth in the modern world is, if anything, acute.

The Stoic tradition captures this with particular clarity. For Epictetus, Seneca, and Marcus Aurelius, the central distinction lay between what lies within our control and what does not. Wisdom began at that boundary. Viewed through such a lens, financial resilience is less about grasping markets or predicting outcomes, and more about mastering responses. Volatility cannot be avoided, but one can shape the way it is met. Compounding cannot be guaranteed, but behaviours can be chosen that give compounding space to work. The fixation on rates, forecasts, or political winds may feel responsible, but in Stoic terms it is wasted energy. Influence lies closer to home: in our habits, convictions, and perspective. Endurance begins, for the Stoic, in sovereignty over the emotions.

Set beside this is the Buddhist orientation, which shifts the focus from control to release. Where Stoicism counsels acceptance, Buddhism advises disentanglement from the craving that warps our dealings with the world. Applied to wealth, it means loosening the knot between money and identity, ambition and agitation, growth and meaning. Detachment is not abdication, nor a retreat into passivity. It is action unburdened by clinging—investing without fixation, building without dread of loss, planning without grasp. The effect is a smoothing of inner turbulence. Presence without obsession. Endurance here emerges not from gritted teeth but from mental clarity. The Buddhist investor is no less active, only less ensnared.

This distinction matters in long horizons. Detachment enables one to weather losses without over-identifying with them, to adapt without collapsing. It cultivates a steadiness not dependent on indices, peers, or fleeting benchmarks. Compounding requires not only sound returns but stamina through dull seasons, uneventful quarters, the monotony of repetition. Detachment shields conviction during those unglamorous stretches.

Taoist philosophy adds another thread: Wu Wei, "non-doing" or effortless action. It is not sloth but alignment—choosing moments when the current favours the boat. The Taoist counsel is against forcing, against excessive interference. In finance, this strikes at the cult of hustle and constant optimisation. The Taoist investor does not chase every rumour or twitch at every chart. They watch, they wait, and act when timing tilts in their favour. It is the difference between effort and efficacy. Between exhausting strain and still effectiveness. Endurance here is not grim defiance but non-interference when interference would harm.

Such a posture harmonises with compounding itself. The greatest financial force thrives when left undisturbed. Constant tinkering, like overwatering, kills the very growth intended. Wu Wei is not esoteric—it is precisely how compounding works: quietly, invisibly, until suddenly visible. Endurance in this sense is less about resistance than about giving time its natural course.

Yet, left in isolation, these traditions risk floating into abstraction or exoticism. The balancing thread comes from Western pragmatism. Here endurance finds a home in method and system. Pragmatism insists on what works—not as slogans, but as processes that outlast moods. Think of Buffett's ordinary routines or Munger's habit of inversion. Their results are not built on rare genius alone, but on the patient repetition of simple, protective behaviours. Strategic monotony.

This pragmatic strand insists that systems surpass goals, process outpaces ambition, and survival matters more than projection. It honours outcomes, but not at the expense of depth. Its wisdom is methodological: avoid unforced errors, minimise variance, endure long enough for asymmetry to tilt rewards your way. Endurance, in this light, is less about heroics and more about showing up reliably, boringly, again and again.

Taken together—Stoic, Buddhist, Taoist, pragmatic—these schools form a kind of architecture for wealth that lasts. Each in its way teaches that the hardest part of compounding is not the mathematics. It is remaining present, coherent, and unshaken through the long, unremarkable stretches where little seems to happen. To stay in the game is itself the rarest discipline.

What follows is not a rulebook but a set of lenses—ways of seeing difficulty, uncertainty, and the slow, unglamorous path of compounding. You need not adopt an ideology; you may simply borrow perspectives. The Stoic lends clarity about control. The Buddhist, freedom from craving. The Taoist, a feel for timing. The pragmatist, the virtue of constancy. These are not curiosities; they are instruments—practical tools for coherence as much as for finance.

To endure is not merely to suffer through. It is to shape behaviour, worldview, and expectation in alignment with reality's deeper rhythms. Reality rewards steadiness, not haste. It honours composure, not agitation. It treasures time, not frantic motion. If we would build wealth that survives—materially, emotionally, philosophically—we must return to these deeper teachings. Ancient though they are, their urgency is not diminished. In fact, in a culture of acceleration, their relevance is keener than ever.

Stoic Wealth: Control What You Can, Release What You Can't

The most powerful investment advice often has nothing to do with markets, timing, or portfolio composition. It lies instead in the art of emotional management—specifically, in the discipline of distinguishing what is within our control from what is not. This deceptively simple mental model, drawn from the Stoic philosophers of ancient Greece and Rome, forms one of the most durable frameworks for long-term financial resilience. Not because it promises wealth, but because it stabilises the person pursuing it. In a culture of noise and narrative, Stoicism does something extraordinary: it repositions wealth as a *practice of control*, not of prediction.

The core of Stoic philosophy rests on a single precept, repeated in various forms across the writings of Epictetus, Marcus Aurelius, and Seneca: focus only on what is within your control. Everything else—outcomes, other people's opinions, the market's fluctuations, the future—is to be acknowledged, respected, but not clung to. In modern investing, this principle is both radical and clarifying. We do not control interest rates, recessions, inflation, or innovation curves. But we do control how we allocate attention, how we respond to loss, and whether we stay anchored to a sound process when others are panicking. *Emotional control, in this light, becomes financial control*—not because it manipulates external outcomes, but because it protects internal coherence when it matters most.

This concept is urgently relevant because modern finance culture encourages precisely the opposite orientation. It rewards prediction, speculation, hot takes, and endless analysis of variables over which the individual has little or no influence. Investors are inundated with commentary—economic forecasts, algorithmic models, geopolitical risks—none of which they can meaningfully affect. The effect is paralysing. Action becomes confused with insight, and energy is spent not on managing behaviour, but on reacting to noise. From a Stoic standpoint, this is a kind of psychological self-harm: attempting to control the uncontrollable while neglecting the one domain we fully command—our own thoughts, actions, and habits.

Consider the market crash of March 2020. Amid unprecedented panic, traders scrambled to make sense of collapsing indices. Algorithms were rewired. Fund managers braced for redemptions. Social media frothed with speculation. Yet the most enduring returns from that period did not come from those who outguessed the system. They came from those who *did nothing irrational.* Investors who stayed invested, who remained aligned to their long-term plans, who refused to act out of fear—these were the individuals who reaped the rewards of emotional composure. From a Stoic perspective, their success was not accidental. It was philosophical. They understood that while they could not dictate the duration or scale of a crash, they could control whether they panicked. That decision, repeated over a lifetime, is what separates transient gains from sustainable wealth.

Marcus Aurelius wrote, *"You have power over your mind—not outside events. Realise this, and you will find strength."* This is not abstract moralism. It is functional insight. To the extent that investors internalise this principle, they reduce reactivity, preserve capital, and allow compounding to do its quiet work. Stoicism, then, is not anti-emotion. It is anti-impulsivity. It acknowledges fear, greed, and hope—but denies them authority. It does not pretend emotions can be removed from decision-making. Rather, it seeks to situate them within a wider context of reasoned agency.

The deeper insight here is that control, in Stoic terms, is not control over outcomes—it is control over *alignment.* Are my actions aligned with my principles? Are my responses proportionate to the signal, or distorted by noise? Have I done the work to distinguish what matters from what merely distracts? These questions are central to both ethical and financial resilience. They turn wealth-building from a technical exercise into a philosophical discipline. Without this lens, even the best strategy can be undone by a bad reaction. The market does not need to beat you. You can beat yourself.

This concept of alignment also changes how we view risk. Stoicism does not promote recklessness or apathy. It encourages risk-taking *within the sphere of reasoned control.* This means making decisions based on process, not predictions. It means accepting volatility without internalising every fluctuation. It means planning for downside without obsessing over it. Seneca famously wrote, *"He who suffers before it is necessary, suffers more than is necessary."* Modern investors would do well to reflect on this when doomscrolling headlines that invite premature anxiety. Much of what we call research is really just forecasting discomfort. A Stoic investor, by contrast, anticipates loss, but does not *live in it.* They build systems that account for uncertainty—then return their focus to execution.

This reorientation is especially powerful in an environment obsessed with performance. Outcome obsession is the modern investor's disease: checking portfolios daily, comparing returns, chasing benchmarks. But Stoicism offers a profound antidote. *Success, in Stoic terms, is defined by the quality of one's actions, not their results.* This is not complacency—it is a commitment to integrity. A long-term investor who followed their plan, stuck to their allocations, rebalanced appropriately, and didn't flinch during a crash has succeeded—regardless of what the market happened to do that year. They acted with clarity, not compulsion. And over time, that is what compounds.

This also means that enduring wealth cannot be separated from enduring character. The same disciplines that govern financial resilience—restraint, presence, humility, temperance—are the disciplines that govern a stable life. Stoicism does not just shape how we allocate capital. It shapes how we allocate *attention,* how we manage energy, how we interpret setbacks. The Stoic investor is not unemotional. They are emotionally literate. They understand that wealth is not built in spreadsheets—it is built in the ability to delay reaction, to sit with uncertainty, and to act when action is prudent, not merely available.

Real-world case studies reinforce this philosophy. Take Jack Bogle, founder of Vanguard and pioneer of the index fund. His innovation was not in finding alpha. It was in rejecting the illusion that alpha could be reliably found. He built a system around what he could control—cost, diversification, discipline—and ignored what he couldn't—short-term movements, market sentiment, the next hot fund manager. His success was not just mathematical. It was Stoic in orientation. He placed principle above prediction. That posture has outperformed a thousand clever forecasts.

Likewise, consider Anne Scheiber, a former IRS auditor who retired in 1944 with $5,000 and died with over $22 million. She never chased trends, sought advice, or changed strategies. She invested patiently, lived modestly, and controlled what she could: costs, time, and temperament. The world barely noticed her—but the system she followed was unshakably sound. This is what Stoic wealth looks like in practice: quiet, persistent, grounded.

The practical takeaway from this is not merely psychological. It is architectural. Your financial system—your asset allocation, savings habits, investment cadence—should be built around what you *can actually manage*, not what you hope to predict. The goal is not to eliminate all uncertainty. The goal is to eliminate unnecessary reactivity. This means removing friction, automating contributions, building buffers, and removing triggers that hijack behaviour. It means simplifying where others are optimising. It means accepting that *a plan you can stick to is always superior to one you will abandon in pursuit of something shinier.*

Stoicism reminds us that emotional mastery is not an accessory to financial success. It is a precondition. Control what you can. Release what you can't. This is not passivity—it is strategic self-possession. In the theatre of modern finance, where every headline demands your attention and every swing of the market tests your nerve, this ancient insight remains not only relevant—but radical. Stoic wealth is not about beating the market. It is about refusing to be beaten by yourself.

The Buddhist View: Detachment and Long-Term Contentment

Modern finance thrives on tension—between now and later, fear and greed, action and restraint. Yet few philosophies offer a more potent counterweight to this churn than Buddhism. Not because it offers a model of investing, but because it presents a radically different model of mind. At the heart of Buddhist teaching lies a counterintuitive yet transformative idea: freedom is found not in grasping outcomes, but in letting them go. For the long-term wealth builder, this principle is not a spiritual abstraction. It is a strategic lens for navigating uncertainty with grace, composure, and internal steadiness.

The Buddhist doctrine of non-attachment is frequently misunderstood. It does not advocate indifference, nor does it imply a rejection of effort, ambition, or worldly activity. Rather, it teaches us to engage fully in action—while loosening our emotional dependency on the results. This is where it intersects with the emotional core of long-term compounding. Investing over time, by its very nature, involves outcomes we cannot control: market returns, interest rates, policy changes, or black swan events. What we *can* control are our responses—whether we react impulsively to short-term volatility or remain anchored in principle. *Non-attachment, then, becomes a form of mental insulation from reactive behaviour.*

To understand how this works in practice, consider the experience of a long-term investor during a bear market. Prices fall, headlines scream, portfolios shrink. The untrained mind, conditioned to avoid discomfort, experiences this as a personal threat. Panic selling often follows—not because the strategy failed, but because the *attachment to outcome* was too tightly wound around short-term expectations. The Buddhist perspective reframes this: discomfort is not a signal to flee, but a signal to examine. Are we reacting from fear? Are we trying to eliminate uncertainty through control? Are we outsourcing our peace of mind to external conditions?

This reflective discipline—staying present without clinging—cultivates a kind of emotional patience that is indispensable for compounding. Wealth rarely grows in straight lines. It advances in fits, reversals, and long periods of perceived stagnation. The investor who expects linear progression is perpetually disappointed, while the investor who detaches from that expectation is liberated to stay the course. *Non-attachment is not apathy—it is realism with composure.*

There is a parallel here with mindfulness meditation, a core Buddhist practice. When thoughts arise—desires, fears, anticipations—the practitioner is taught to observe without judgment and return to the breath. Investing offers a similar challenge. Markets provoke constant mental chatter: should I shift allocations, chase this sector, hedge against that forecast? Each thought demands a response. Yet the most successful investors often do something deceptively simple: *they notice the noise, but don't act on it.* This is mindfulness applied to capital. It is the skill of returning to the breath of your long-term plan, again and again, despite distraction.

This approach also cultivates contentment—not as complacency, but as emotional self-sufficiency. Buddhism teaches that suffering arises from craving—the insatiable "more" that characterises much of Western consumerism and short-term speculation. The investor who always wants more yield, faster growth, or constant upside becomes easy prey for risk. Chasing novelty replaces clarity. Contentment, by contrast, allows the investor to stay with what is working, even when it is not exciting. It fosters the discipline to accumulate slowly, incrementally, and with humility. *There is power in accepting enough*—in recognising that peace of mind is not found in perpetual gain, but in emotional groundedness through all seasons.

The philosophy also offers tools for recovering from loss. Buddhism does not deny suffering; it builds a framework for how to meet it. Every investor will, at some point, face drawdowns, errors, or missed opportunities. The attachment to being right, to perfect timing, or to uninterrupted success creates unnecessary psychological burden. Buddhist detachment invites us to experience these moments fully, but not personally. A market downturn is not a verdict on your worth. A failed trade is not a reflection of your intelligence. *Events are what they are; suffering is how we interpret them.* The less we fuse identity with performance, the more resilient we become.

Consider, too, the relevance of impermanence—another central Buddhist idea. Everything is in flux: economies, asset classes, personal goals. The Buddhist does not fear this; they expect it. From this view, volatility is not a problem to be fixed but a condition to be accepted. This aligns perfectly with the psychology of long-term investing. Every financial plan must withstand change. Non-attachment allows us to adapt without losing balance, to evolve strategies without abandoning principles. It tempers the rigidity that so often leads to overreaction. When one does not insist that things must go a certain way, one remains open to wiser responses when they do not.

A powerful real-world illustration of this mindset is found in the story of the Japanese firm Shiseido. After decades of methodical growth, the company weathered multiple recessions without engaging in massive layoffs or short-term restructuring. Their executives, influenced by Zen Buddhism, focused on endurance, community, and long-term reputation over quarterly profits. This ethos—quiet resilience over reactive speed—produced not just economic durability but cultural loyalty. Their wealth was not only financial; it was relational and reputational, compounding silently over time.

We might contrast this with the mindset of day traders or meme stock speculators, whose success depends almost entirely on the ability to act quickly on emotion, trend, or hype. These are systems built on attachment—to momentum, to instant returns, to social validation. And while they may generate dramatic headlines, they rarely produce enduring outcomes. The Buddhist investor, by contrast, is indifferent to momentary highs and lows. Their identity is not constructed around performance. Their equanimity is an advantage, precisely because it is so rare.

Importantly, detachment is not passive. Buddhism does not advise the abdication of responsibility, only the release of obsession. One can act decisively without being consumed by results. One can plan diligently without believing that the plan guarantees peace. This balance—of intention without fixation—is what enables sustained action without burnout. In financial terms, it means automating savings, revisiting allocations thoughtfully, and reviewing plans periodically, without falling into the trap of micromanagement. The market may change, but the posture remains the same: alert, calm, and unattached.

The modern investor operates in a world that relentlessly encourages attachment. Every advertisement, social feed, and earnings report is designed to trigger desire, urgency, or fear. The Buddhist path offers something far more radical: stillness in motion. It invites the practitioner to show up fully, participate in the world, make decisions with care—and let go. The paradox is that such detachment often produces better outcomes, not worse. When we are not hijacked by craving, we make better decisions. When we are not paralysed by fear, we stay invested. When we are not obsessed with now, we allow time to do its deepest work.

The long arc of compounding requires an emotional posture few are trained to hold. The Buddhist framework offers not just an ethical worldview, but a practical model for that posture: non-attachment, mindful engagement, and peace with impermanence. These are not exotic spiritual ideals—they are durable tools for anyone seeking to build wealth that lasts. Not just financial wealth, but mental clarity, emotional calm, and behavioural consistency. And those, more than any metric, are the true indicators of financial wisdom.

The Taoist Flow: Acting Without Forcing

The modern world rewards those who appear to push hardest—those who hustle, strive, and broadcast their effort as proof of worth. We live in an age that equates force with effectiveness. Yet for thousands of years, Taoist philosophy has taught something radically different: that the most powerful actions are often the ones that appear the most effortless. This principle, known as *Wu Wei*, is not a call to passivity, but an invitation to participate in life and decision-making without resistance, excessive control, or egoic imposition. In the context of wealth-building, Wu Wei challenges the dominant paradigm of constant striving and offers a sophisticated framework for cultivating financial endurance through presence, timing, and intuitive alignment.

At the heart of Taoism is the concept of *the Tao*—a term translated loosely as "the Way," referring to the natural order of the universe. The Tao is not a god or doctrine, but a pattern, a current of unfolding that governs all life. Wu Wei, literally translated as "non-action" or more accurately "non-forced action," refers to behaviour that is in harmony with this pattern. It is a mode of action that flows rather than fights. In practice, it looks like choosing the right moment rather than acting at any cost, and trusting that things develop best when we do not constantly interfere.

To understand the relevance of Wu Wei to wealth-building, consider the behaviour of experienced long-term investors. They are not in a state of constant activity. They do not trade compulsively, check market dashboards hourly, or obsess over every data point. They act when necessary and remain still when that serves better. Their posture is more akin to that of a gardener than a gambler: prepare the soil, plant wisely, water consistently, and resist the urge to dig up the roots. *The results are not willed into being—they are allowed to emerge through patience, positioning, and respect for time.*

Contrast this with the psychology of day traders, speculative flippers, or market chasers. Their entire mindset is built on intervention. Every tick in the chart demands a response. Every rumour becomes a call to action. Their energy is consumed in reaction rather than reflection. Yet data overwhelmingly shows that such hyperactivity correlates not with superior returns but with increased volatility, lower performance, and heightened stress. This is not strategy. It is compulsion masquerading as productivity. Wu Wei invites us to see the difference.

Importantly, Wu Wei does not suggest doing *nothing*. It demands a refinement of effort—right timing, right proportion, right motivation. In Taoist thought, the oak tree bends in the storm not because it is weak, but because it is wise. The water flows around the rock not because it gives up, but because it endures. This philosophy aligns remarkably well with what behavioural finance now confirms: that restraint, not reaction, is often the highest form of intelligence in complex systems. Financial markets, like natural ecosystems, reward those who observe patterns and adapt subtly, not those who impose their will with rigid insistence.

This ethos of flow also intersects with the increasingly studied concept of *deep patience*—a discipline not of sitting still indefinitely, but of responding only when the conditions align. Consider the case of Warren Buffett, whose investment philosophy embodies a modern Wu Wei. Buffett is famous not only for what he buys, but for how long he waits to buy it. Years may pass before he deploys capital. He does not act for the sake of movement. He acts when the Tao—the economic current—presents an opportunity that fits naturally within his values and strategy. This is not hesitation; it is harmony.

The applicability of Wu Wei extends beyond markets into the emotional domain of wealth. So much financial suffering arises from attempts to control the uncontrollable: predicting recessions, timing booms, securing absolute certainty. These desires are rooted in the ego's need for dominance. But wealth, especially lasting wealth, is not created through domination. It is built through relationship—with time, with uncertainty, with broader systems that move independently of our will. *To practice Wu Wei is to trade control for attunement. And that shift, though subtle, changes everything.*

There is also a psychological benefit. Those who practise acting without forcing tend to experience less anxiety and burnout. Constant striving generates not only fatigue but a subtle belief that nothing is ever enough. Every goal reached births a new one. Every milestone achieved becomes a new metric to outperform. This treadmill of striving is a recipe for restlessness. Wu Wei, by contrast, offers a state of internal alignment where decisions feel right rather than forced, and results are accepted rather than wrestled into existence.

Practical examples of this abound in the business world. Take the case of Patagonia, whose leadership practices could be described as Taoist in character. The company avoids short-term profit maximisation in favour of long-term ecological and social alignment. Its decisions often seem slow or countercultural—opting out of Black Friday sales, closing stores to encourage civic engagement, or making supply chain decisions based on environmental principles rather than margins. Yet this approach has not led to mediocrity. Quite the opposite: Patagonia enjoys fierce brand loyalty, steady profitability, and an enviable culture. Their "non-forced" approach has proven more resilient than many competitors' aggressive strategies.

We must also recognise that Wu Wei is a posture that must be trained. For those raised in the ideology of hustle, slowing down can feel like negligence. Choosing not to act can provoke guilt. Letting go of outcome obsession may feel like weakness. But that discomfort is not a sign of failure. It is a sign that our nervous systems have been conditioned to confuse urgency with importance. Like meditation, the practice of Wu Wei requires repetition. We must unlearn reflex and relearn rhythm.

The discipline of non-forcing is particularly relevant in times of volatility. When markets wobble or uncertainty strikes, the instinct is often to intervene, "fix" the problem, or find an immediate solution. But the Taoist would advise: pause. Is your action grounded in clarity or compulsion? Is it in alignment with your values or a reaction to fear? Is it sustainable or merely dramatic? These questions do not delay progress. They deepen it. *The decision not to act is itself a decision—one that protects the fragile process of long-term growth.*

A final insight from Taoism is this: nature never hurries, yet everything is accomplished. Compounding is itself a Taoist principle in disguise. It works not through bursts, but through consistency. Not through stress, but through structure. The compounding of wealth mirrors the compounding of water carving stone—not because it tried harder, but because it stayed the course. The lesson for us is clear: the more we learn to act in harmony with the larger flow—of markets, cycles, systems—the less we need to force, and the more we can trust.

Acting without forcing is not about doing less. It is about doing *right.* It is the art of efficient effort, of engaged patience, of choosing our moments with precision rather than panic. It is a deeply intelligent, deeply humane way to engage with uncertainty. And in a culture addicted to speed, noise, and hustle, it offers an antidote that is both timeless and urgently relevant. Wu Wei is not the absence of ambition—it is ambition refined by wisdom. And that, more than any tactic, is what endures.

Western Pragmatism: The Compounding Mindset

If there is a single principle that quietly governs wealth creation yet is dramatically underappreciated in mainstream financial culture, it is this: compounding rewards not intensity but consistency. The Western mind, shaped by industrial speed and technological scale, often romanticises explosive growth—overnight success, unicorn startups, market timing, and big wins. But when you trace the actual architecture of enduring wealth, from generational fortunes to personal financial independence, the curve bends toward something much less glamorous and infinitely more sustainable: *accumulation over time.* And that requires a mindset—not of heroics, but of daily alignment.

The compounding mindset is the financial expression of Western pragmatism. It is not animated by utopian dreams or philosophical abstraction but by tangible, repeatable action. It holds that real progress is built incrementally. It recognises that outcomes are rarely the result of a single brilliant move and almost always the result of small, disciplined decisions repeated over long spans. This idea may be rooted in logic and evidence, but to adopt it fully requires a profound behavioural shift. Because while the mathematics of compounding are simple, the psychology of staying the course—especially when the world celebrates drama—is anything but.

The most powerful expression of this mindset in modern financial history is Warren Buffett. The statistics are often quoted, but the implications rarely internalised. Over 95% of Buffett's wealth was earned after his 65th birthday. Not because he changed strategies late in life, but because he had the patience to keep doing the same thing for over half a century. *The secret is not superior intellect. It is behavioural endurance.* And yet, for all the books written about him, most investors still fail to model what made him successful—not stock selection, but time in the game.

Western pragmatism, at its best, is deeply aligned with this ethos. It values what works. It de-emphasises ideology in favour of empirical evidence. It does not confuse movement with progress. In this way, it mirrors the Eastern philosophical traditions explored earlier in this chapter—but with its own vocabulary. Where Taoism speaks of effortless action and Buddhism of detachment, Western pragmatism speaks of process, margin of safety, compounding, and durability. The terms may differ, but the orientation is remarkably similar: *trust the process, not the moment.*

The American philosopher William James once wrote that truth is what works in practice. In finance, what works in practice is not what's loudest, flashiest, or most viral—it is what survives. And what survives are behaviours, habits, and decisions that produce resilience under stress. The compounding mindset is not a get-rich formula; it is a stay-rich principle. It is less concerned with maximising returns than with avoiding ruin. It prizes longevity above excitement. That orientation is its strength and its challenge.

In a culture wired for immediacy, compounding requires an almost countercultural posture. Social media platforms reward short-term attention; markets amplify short-term noise; economic cycles tempt short-term trades. The environment conspires against stillness. But the compounding mindset rejects the illusion that success is a sprint. It builds routines that operate independent of mood. It treats setbacks as noise, not verdicts. And perhaps most importantly, it accepts boredom—not as a failure of engagement, but as a feature of mastery.

Consider the systems thinkers who designed modern investing tools like dollar-cost averaging or target-date retirement funds. These are not built for optimisation in the narrow sense; they are built for emotional discipline. They are designed to remove friction, reduce impulsivity, and automate the compounding effect through behaviourally sound structures. The brilliance lies not in complexity but in humility. *They assume the investor is human and fallible—and win by designing around it.*

This same logic has been adopted by enduring businesses. Look at Costco. It does not chase market fads, launch risky ventures, or glamorise disruption. Its model is brutally simple: offer consistent value, treat customers fairly, and reinvest in efficiency. Over decades, this unsexy discipline has delivered better shareholder returns than many tech darlings. Or take Southwest Airlines—long a case study in consistent strategy and restrained growth. These companies understand a truth most markets forget: that the most potent form of leverage is *time applied to soundness*, not risk applied to opportunity.

The compounding mindset also demands a redefinition of what counts as "success." It invites us to focus less on spectacular gains and more on sustained progress. That means tracking behaviours, not just balances. Are you saving consistently? Investing steadily? Managing risk with clarity? These are the drivers of durable wealth. Yet they rarely appear in the narratives that dominate financial media, which favour headlines over habits.

Here lies the practical challenge: how do we train ourselves to value what isn't immediately gratifying? The answer lies not in willpower, but in systems. Build friction into bad decisions. Automate the right ones. Create feedback loops that reward process. Remove exposure to noise. Set default behaviours that reflect long-term goals. *This is not productivity advice—it is emotional infrastructure for financial sustainability.*

There is also a deeper ethical current in this thinking. Compounding respects future value. It asks us to honour the person we will be decades from now. It resists the cultural norm of extraction—taking everything now and leaving nothing for later. In this sense, the compounding mindset is not just a financial stance but a moral one. It assumes continuity. It affirms stewardship. It prioritises legacy over leverage.

The most impressive compounding stories are rarely public. They belong to quiet professionals who consistently invest in pensions, to families that prioritise savings over spending, to small businesses that reinvest earnings rather than chase scale. These stories don't make headlines—but they shape lives. Their wealth is not visible in any one transaction. It's visible in what it makes possible over time: freedom, margin, peace.

Even within entrepreneurship—a domain often synonymous with risk-taking—the compounding mindset is increasingly relevant. Founders who succeed over decades (rather than months) understand that product-market fit is not a singular discovery but an evolving discipline. They iterate steadily, manage burn rates prudently, and cultivate teams with emotional longevity. Their success is not built on gamble but on *compounding trust, compounding skill, compounding insight.*

To embrace this mindset is to embrace limitations—of time, energy, and willpower. It is to accept that we cannot win through force or brilliance alone. But it is also to access a deeper form of strength: the strength of consistency. Of showing up. Of small wins that become irreversible. And that strength, though invisible in the moment, eventually becomes unstoppable.

The compounding mindset is not merely a financial concept. It is a worldview. It says that what matters most happens slowly. That value accrues beneath the surface. That repetition is not failure—it is mastery in motion. And in a world addicted to the extraordinary, that belief is not just rare. It is revolutionary.

Chapter 4
Emotional Capital: The Real Balance Sheet of the Wealthy

At the root of every durable fortune lies a resource seldom named, rarely quantified, and almost never taught in schools of finance. It does not appear on balance sheets, nor is it tracked by the analysts who obsess over quarterly returns. Yet it is this hidden reserve that separates the fleeting from the lasting. That resource is emotional capital: the strength to stay composed under pressure, to move consistently through uncertainty, and to resist one's own worst impulses precisely when temptation and panic collide. It is not a quirk of psychology. It is the ground upon which financial longevity is built.

Much of financial education begins with the external: the mechanics of assets, liabilities, interest, and returns. But it is the internal terrain from which choices emerge that decides whether those mechanics yield fruit or ruin. Emotional capital is unlike monetary capital in one crucial respect—it cannot be borrowed, outsourced, or quickly restored. It must be earned and safeguarded. And when it runs dry, the costs are immediate and unforgiving. Market corrections, career setbacks, liquidity squeezes—these rarely destroy people through lack of opportunity or intelligence. More often, they are undone by a drained capacity to hold steady. The investor who capitulates to panic, the entrepreneur seduced by the latest fad, the executive blinded by overextension—each is defeated not by circumstance but by a deficit of inner reserves.

What this chapter attempts is a serious excavation of that inner reserve. Emotional capital is no invention of modern finance; Stoics and sages have long spoken of its weight. But in an age of perpetual distraction, economic whiplash, and algorithmically engineered fear, the requirement for it has sharpened. Impulsivity is punished swiftly now. Markets exploit fear with clinical precision. Platforms amplify envy until even ordinary progress feels like failure. To hold a long view, to remain unreactive, to execute with patience—such behaviours have become more than sound strategy; they are, in fact, acts of cultural rebellion.

The paradox lies here: emotional capital feels intangible, yet its impact is concrete. The gap between the investor who dumps assets in a 20% downturn and the one who calmly rebalances is not explained by intellect. It is explained by inner ballast. The latter does not win by superior foresight, but by superior self-regulation. Each act of restraint becomes a kind of invisible deposit. Each moment of composure in chaos compounds into long-term advantage.

Look closely at those remembered as great investors, entrepreneurs, and operators. Their defining trait is not flamboyant genius but emotional endurance. Ray Dalio built his fortune not on clairvoyant predictions alone, but on a discipline of reflection, system-building, and detachment from outcomes. Benjamin Graham's margin-of-safety principle was never merely arithmetic—it was behavioural armour. He designed frameworks that could withstand irrationality, including his own. Their brilliance was not purely intellectual—it was behavioural engineering.

This chapter will revisit such profiles. From the investors who sidestepped the dot-com mania by clinging to discipline, to the family businesses that chose steady profitability over reckless scaling, to households that stayed the course through recessionary storms—the through-line is evident. Their strength lay in cultivated temperament, not tactical wizardry.

Yet recognising emotional capital is only the beginning. The deeper work is cultivation. As muscle grows under resistance, so too does this capital expand under practice. Habits of probabilistic thinking, reframing uncertainty, even learning to tolerate boredom—these are exercises. So too is designing an environment that trims noise and simplifies decisions. Philosophical anchors—whether Stoic, Buddhist, or pragmatic—become structural supports. None of these are glamorous, and none are shortcuts. But they accumulate, just as compounding capital does, through repetition.

This also demands a reframing of what financial preparedness means. Net worth, while important, is no predictor of resilience in crisis. One may have ample liquidity yet collapse in panic. High yield cannot offset chronic anxiety. True readiness lies in the ability to stay principled in the troughs: to remain invested through drawdowns, to keep perspective through envy, to wait through underperformance. The balance sheet that matters most is internal.

It is worth stressing: emotional capital is not an absence of fear. It is the capacity to feel fear without surrendering to it. Not stoicism in the caricatured sense of suppression, but in the classical sense of proportion. The emotionally wealthy still tremble at uncertainty; they simply do not act from it. They see hysteria without joining it. They take losses without abandoning their framework. That detachment is not indifference. It is discipline. And discipline, unlike access or raw talent, can be learned.

There is, too, a cultural critique buried in this idea. Finance, as currently structured, idolises metrics and models. These matter. Yet even the best model collapses under strain if its operator cannot hold it steady. An imperfect plan, executed with emotional consistency, outperforms a perfect plan abandoned in panic. Few institutions train this. Fewer individuals do—until chaos exposes the gap.

Here the notion of emotional reserves deserves emphasis. Just as emergency funds buffer shocks, emotional liquidity cushions behavioural collapse. How much ambiguity can you endure without deviation? How many losses can you absorb without breaking stride? How long can you toil without external recognition? These are not philosophical puzzles but stress tests of one's behavioural scaffolding.

Emotional capital is not static. It can be trained. And its growth curve resembles that of financial capital itself: incremental, slow, then exponential. Each time you resist reaction, you widen your advantage. Each time you act from principle under duress, you strengthen neural grooves that hold you later. The market never sends you a statement of these gains, but they shape every statement it does.

If financial capital is what you possess, emotional capital is how long you can keep it. It is the shield against wounds you might otherwise inflict on yourself. It is the solvent for panic. It is the silent force beneath rational action in irrational times. And it may well be the most consequential asset of all—not because it promises returns, but because it ensures you endure long enough to receive them.

What Is Emotional Capital?

The most devastating losses in finance are rarely caused by faulty mathematics, mispriced assets, or bad luck. They stem from human behaviour. Not behaviour in abstract, but specific moments when emotions override logic—when fear eclipses long-term thinking, or when greed dismantles discipline. It is in those moments that fortunes are made or lost, not on balance sheets but inside people. And what governs these moments is a resource rarely quantified in financial literature: *emotional capital.*

Emotional capital is the capacity to withstand uncertainty, resist reactive decisions, and remain aligned with sound strategy in the face of volatility. It is a measure not of how much you know or how much you have, but how well you can execute what you know under psychological strain. It is the behavioural buffer between principle and panic, between plan and deviation. And it is arguably the most underappreciated determinant of financial endurance.

Most wealth-building frameworks focus on external capital: human capital (skills), financial capital (assets), and social capital (networks). But emotional capital sits upstream from all three. Without it, skills become underutilised, assets get mismanaged, and relationships are strained by impulsive decisions. A trader may have brilliant insights but crumble under pressure. A business owner may abandon strategy for fads. A salaried professional may sell their investments during a temporary drawdown, confusing discomfort with danger. Each of these scenarios reflects not a failure of intelligence, but a shortage of emotional bandwidth.

Consider two investors with identical portfolios during a sharp market correction. One experiences discomfort but continues contributing monthly, maintaining their strategic allocations. The other panics, liquidates their holdings at a loss, and later re-enters the market at higher prices. On paper, both had equal opportunity. In practice, the one with greater emotional capital outperformed—not by predicting markets, but by managing their internal state more effectively. *Behavioural divergence created financial divergence.* And that divergence compounds over decades.

Emotional capital operates much like financial capital: it grows through disciplined contributions, it can be depleted by poor decisions, and it offers compounding returns to those who preserve it. The individual who can navigate volatility without emotional exhaustion accumulates long-term advantage. Not in dramatic bursts, but through steady, principled action in the face of temptation and turbulence.

It is important to distinguish emotional capital from generic resilience or optimism. Resilience is the ability to recover; emotional capital is the ability to stay steady enough that recovery is unnecessary. Optimism may fuel risk-taking, but without emotional regulation, that optimism becomes reckless. Emotional capital doesn't deny emotion—it integrates it. It recognises fear, greed, envy, and regret as natural forces, then builds the cognitive infrastructure to act *despite* them.

This internal infrastructure is often what separates first-generation wealth builders from those who struggle to maintain it. Those who accumulate wealth from modest beginnings often do so through extreme diligence and delayed gratification. But once the volatility of real wealth management sets in—asset fluctuations, public scrutiny, business cycles—only those with sufficient emotional capital can hold course. Without it, people succumb to the paradox of abundance: the more you have, the more you fear losing it. Wealth becomes a source of anxiety, not freedom.

Even professional investors are not immune. Take the example of Bill Ackman during the COVID-19 crash of March 2020. In a 28-minute CNBC interview, he publicly aired his fear that "hell is coming," causing a temporary panic. Meanwhile, other investors—such as Howard Marks—advised calm, measured thinking. Both were intelligent. Both had deep expertise. But their emotional posture shaped their messaging, their actions, and their reputations. The contrast was not intellectual; it was emotional.

Or consider the entrepreneur who scales a business during a bull market, only to panic during a revenue downturn, pivot chaotically, and burn cash on reactive strategies. They blame the economy, the team, or timing. But often the root cause is internal: the inability to sit with discomfort long enough for thoughtful decisions to emerge. *When emotional capital is low, volatility is not endured—it is personalised.* Every dip feels like doom. Every setback feels like identity failure. Decisions become defensive, not strategic.

To clarify: emotional capital is not stoicism-as-suppression. It is not the absence of feeling. It is the *ability to experience intense emotional stimuli without collapsing into impulsive action.* This distinction matters. Many people suppress fear until it erupts. They posture confidence until overexposure breaks them. Emotional capital allows one to be honest about emotional weather while remaining unswayed by it. It permits honesty without hysteria.

The psychological literature offers insights into how emotional capital forms. Cognitive behavioural therapy (CBT), mindfulness-based stress reduction (MBSR), and exposure therapy all share a common aim: increase the subject's ability to remain present with discomfort without overreacting. In investing, this might look like reading one's portfolio statement during a market dip and choosing to stay the course. In entrepreneurship, it could mean sitting with stagnant growth without making impulsive structural changes. These micro-moments accumulate. Over time, they become the architecture of durable inner stability.

Philosophical traditions have long understood this. The Stoics spoke of *apatheia*—a state of equanimity that arises from clear perception and detachment from externals. The Bhagavad Gita calls for *samatvam*—evenness of mind in gain and loss. Buddhism teaches the cultivation of *upekkha*—equanimity through non-attachment. All point to the same idea: *emotional sovereignty is the highest form of mastery*—and the hardest to measure.

But the lack of measurement doesn't make emotional capital any less real. On the contrary, its invisibility makes it more dangerous when absent. Financial media doesn't display a "fear index" next to market quotes that accurately captures what individual investors are feeling. No brokerage account shows "panic risk" or "patience depletion." Yet these are the forces that drive most real-world losses. The 2008 crisis, the dot-com bust, the crypto bubbles—all featured not just economic shocks, but widespread emotional capitulation. Markets didn't fall because models failed—they fell because humans did.

One might ask: can emotional capital be developed intentionally? The answer is unequivocally yes. It begins with awareness—recognising your emotional triggers and typical responses under stress. Then comes training: deliberately placing yourself in controlled discomfort and practising non-reactivity. That might include simulation exercises, journaling during periods of uncertainty, or rehearsing mental models that prioritise principle over impulse. It may involve building a community that reinforces patience, or designing decision environments that reduce reactive stimuli. Over time, these practices reinforce neural patterns that favour stability.

This also raises the question of measurement. If emotional capital is so important, why is it rarely tracked? One reason is that it doesn't fit easily into conventional metrics. You cannot backtest emotional resilience. It doesn't appear in quarterly earnings. But that is no excuse to ignore it. Just because something is hard to quantify does not make it less consequential. On the contrary, it makes it more vital to understand experientially.

A useful way to think about emotional capital is to borrow from risk management frameworks. Consider a "drawdown buffer"—a mental allocation of how much distress you can tolerate before your decision-making degrades. Those with high emotional capital have a wide buffer. They can endure larger losses, longer plateaus, and greater uncertainty without altering their course. Those with low emotional capital are perpetually at risk of self-sabotage, even in minor setbacks. The goal is not to eliminate risk, but to inoculate oneself against its emotional impact.

Ultimately, the serious pursuit of wealth must include the cultivation of emotional capital as a primary practice. It is what allows plans to survive pressure. It is what allows discipline to outlast distraction. And it is what allows time—the ultimate compounding force—to work uninterrupted. Without it, even the most brilliant strategies collapse. With it, even modest plans can thrive. Because *wealth is not just about surviving volatility—it's about not being undone by it.* Emotional capital is what makes that possible.

The Fragility of the Emotionally Poor

The most consistent predictor of long-term financial failure is not bad information, market timing errors, or lack of education—it is the inability to remain composed under psychological pressure. While financial literacy may explain the 'how' of wealth building, emotional resilience explains the 'if'. Emotional poverty is not a deficit of feelings, but a chronic vulnerability to them. It is what makes rational people abandon rational plans, usually at the exact moment when commitment would have paid off. This fragility is not evenly distributed across populations—it correlates not with intelligence or income, but with one's internal ability to metabolise discomfort.

Financial volatility exposes emotional fragility in a way few other forces do. Volatility demands tolerance of ambiguity, discomfort, and delayed rewards. For the emotionally poor—those with little psychological surplus—each market fluctuation feels like a referendum on personal security. Their time horizon collapses. Their reasoning narrows. They react not to the facts of the situation, but to their affective state in the face of it. A ten percent drawdown becomes a crisis. A missed opportunity becomes a perceived failure. A correction becomes confirmation that they were "never meant" for investing. And so they retreat—selling early, chasing safety, or replacing a long-term plan with short-term reactionism.

This behaviour is not irrational in isolation—it's emotionally rational. If an investor's emotional reserves are insufficient to tolerate discomfort, then selling to relieve anxiety makes perfect sense. But it is precisely this *short-term emotional relief* that compounds into *long-term financial erosion.* Every premature exit, every fear-driven allocation, every trend-chasing detour is a tax paid not to the market, but to one's inability to sit still with discomfort. Emotional fragility monetises itself through bad decisions.

Take the behaviour of retail investors during the COVID-19 market crash in March 2020. The S&P 500 dropped roughly 34% in a matter of weeks. The emotionally fragile didn't wait to understand the macroeconomic implications or reassess their portfolio's underlying fundamentals. They sold en masse, moved to cash, and vowed never to "gamble" in the markets again. Those with higher emotional capital—who maintained their composure and rebalanced as needed—were rewarded within months, as markets recovered with historic speed. The divergence in outcome was not about better information; it was about emotional threshold.

The emotionally poor also tend to gravitate towards highly reactive financial strategies—day trading, options speculation, crypto volatility—under the illusion that more control over transactions equals more control over outcomes. But these environments demand even higher emotional capital, not less. The irony is sharp: the people least equipped to handle rapid gains and losses often place themselves in the most emotionally demanding arenas. And when inevitable losses occur, they internalise failure as personal inadequacy, fuelling a cycle of shame and further impulsivity. Markets become a mirror for their own instability.

Compounding this is the cultural encouragement of reactive behaviours. Social media thrives on immediacy. Financial headlines amplify noise over signal. Influencers push emotionally charged narratives—"this is your last chance," "don't miss out," "if you're not making six figures from your side hustle, you're falling behind." All of this erodes emotional capital. It convinces people that patience is naivety and that restraint is weakness. In such an environment, emotional fragility is not just a liability—it becomes a default state.

This fragility also expresses itself in envy. The emotionally poor compare their trajectory not to their own benchmarks, but to the highlight reels of others. If a friend doubles their portfolio in a meme-stock rally, the emotionally fragile feel left behind—even if their own strategy is sound and sustainable. They abandon what works in favour of what feels exciting. They equate activity with intelligence. And they fail to distinguish temporary noise from durable signal. This is how fortunes are diluted—not through catastrophe, but through small, repeated compromises made under the weight of emotional urgency.

It is worth noting that emotional fragility is not always visible. It can hide behind sophistication. Some of the most erratic investors are also the most articulate. They can explain a discounted cash flow model while simultaneously panic-selling a high-quality asset after one bad earnings quarter. Their technical knowledge masks a lack of emotional infrastructure. Conversely, some of the most emotionally resilient investors are unsophisticated by traditional standards—but they stay the course, ignore noise, and trust their process. Over time, this steadiness compounds into significant advantage.

The emotionally poor are not limited to individual investors. Institutions can behave this way too—fund managers who overtrade to appease anxious stakeholders, CEOs who abandon long-term strategy for quarterly appeasement, or boards that overcorrect at the first sign of activist pressure. These are examples of organisational fragility—systems that lack the emotional margin to absorb uncertainty without distortion. The difference between a durable firm and a brittle one often lies in its capacity for calm decision-making under fire.

Nor is emotional poverty fixed. It can be cultivated or depleted over time, based on habits, environments, and choices. Someone raised in a household where money was always a source of tension may enter adulthood with heightened financial sensitivity. Without conscious effort, they will overreact to normal volatility, treat setbacks as catastrophes, and sabotage compounding by constantly course-correcting. But with practice, self-awareness, and structured decision-making frameworks, emotional capital can grow. The fragile can become composed.

This has profound implications for financial education. Traditional curricula focus on budgeting, investing, and risk tolerance—all vital. But they often ignore the emotional layer that governs real-world execution. A person may know what a diversified portfolio is and still sell it all during a downturn. They may understand dollar-cost averaging and still halt contributions when headlines turn negative. Without emotional scaffolding, knowledge collapses under pressure. *The goal, then, is not just to educate—but to fortify.*

To do so requires tools and disciplines. Journaling during periods of volatility to separate fact from feeling. Pre-committing to rebalancing strategies to avoid in-the-moment hesitation. Practising mindfulness to reduce emotional reactivity. Creating decision checklists that prioritise process over impulse. Studying one's past reactions to identify patterns of fragility. Building a community that rewards patience, not performance theatre. These are not soft skills—they are foundational capacities that protect wealth from its most dangerous threat: the person who owns it.

Understanding the fragility of the emotionally poor is not about condescension—it is about recognising a human vulnerability that cuts across class, intelligence, and profession. It invites empathy, not judgment. But it also demands responsibility. Because emotional poverty is costly, not just for individuals, but for families, communities, and societies. It leads to short-termism in policy, volatility in markets, and misallocation of capital across time.

To build emotional capital, we must first acknowledge where it is lacking. And we must replace shame with structure. Because what appears to be personal failure is often a systemic absence of training. The emotionally fragile were not taught to think in decades, to separate identity from portfolio performance, or to respect the role of silence in decision-making. But these are teachable. And in a world that increasingly rewards noise, the capacity for quiet durability becomes a superpower.

Those who build this capacity don't merely survive volatility—they weaponise it. They buy when others are selling. They hold when others are doubting. They thrive not because they are fearless, but because they have rehearsed composure. They are not emotionally perfect—they are emotionally prepared. And over time, this preparation reveals its value not in headlines, but in net worth. Because *emotional strength is the soil in which financial endurance grows*. And fragility, left unchecked, ensures that no strategy—no matter how brilliant—can bear fruit.

Case Studies: The Calm Outperformers

The most valuable trait in investing and entrepreneurship is rarely technical. It isn't prescience, mathematical prowess, or strategic genius. It is the capacity to remain composed when others unravel. Across markets and industries, a small but consistent subset of individuals have demonstrated extraordinary success by doing something deceptively simple: not panicking. Their portfolios compound quietly not because they outrun risk, but because they remain anchored when it strikes. These are the calm outperformers—men and women whose emotional steadiness became the cornerstone of enduring wealth.

Consider John Bogle, founder of Vanguard and father of the index fund revolution. Bogle didn't build his legacy through aggressive plays or flashy predictions. He did it by promoting a principle that almost sounded boring: buy a diversified portfolio of low-cost index funds and *hold them for decades.* During the 2000 dot-com bubble, Bogle was mocked for resisting speculative tech mania. During the 2008 financial crisis, he refused to sell into the panic. Even as passive investing was dismissed as naive by Wall Street's elite, he stuck to his thesis. Why? Because Bogle's temperament was not swayed by noise. His conviction was anchored not in momentary data, but in fundamental belief—and that belief was filtered through emotional restraint. Vanguard now manages over $8 trillion in assets. The calmness that underpinned his choices generated an outcome that aggression alone could never have replicated.

In a very different domain, look at Warren Buffett. His investment decisions are often lauded for their intelligence, but intelligence alone cannot explain his consistency. What separates Buffett is his emotional discipline. He has famously said that temperament is more important than IQ in investing—and his own career proves the point. During the 1973–74 market crash, Buffett continued buying undervalued companies while others liquidated in fear. In the aftermath of the 2008 crisis, he invested billions in firms like Goldman Sachs and Bank of America when the financial world seemed on the brink of collapse. In each instance, the strategy didn't hinge on forecasting—it hinged on *not flinching*. Buffett's long-standing holding of companies like Coca-Cola, American Express, and Apple was not merely a financial act; it was an emotional one. He trusted the underlying value through volatility. That is emotional capital at work: the ability to withstand uncertainty without self-sabotage.

Outside public markets, Sara Blakely, the founder of Spanx, offers a compelling entrepreneurial case. Starting with $5,000 in savings and no formal business training, she grew Spanx into a billion-dollar brand. What's remarkable isn't merely the scale of her success, but her tolerance for ambiguity and rejection. Blakely endured years of being ignored by male investors, laughed out of boardrooms, and repeatedly told the idea was unviable. Yet she kept iterating, adjusting quietly, and holding her ground. Her refusal to let external discouragement destabilise her internal commitment was a display of emotional strength. She stayed the course not because the path was clear, but because she developed the capacity to tolerate the fog.

Ray Dalio, founder of Bridgewater Associates, experienced a public collapse in 1982 after wrongly predicting a global depression. The mistake nearly destroyed his firm. But rather than abandoning his method, Dalio did something rare: he examined his thinking, rebuilt his framework, and trained himself to respond differently to being wrong. The lesson wasn't just epistemological—it was emotional. He rewired how he related to uncertainty. Dalio's emphasis on radical transparency and principled decision-making emerged from this low point. Bridgewater eventually became the world's largest hedge fund. The defining pivot was not technical correction—it was emotional evolution. Calm was not his starting point, but his transformation.

Even in high-volatility environments like venture capital, emotional steadiness has been the differentiator. Chris Sacca, one of the earliest investors in Twitter and Uber, was known less for his predictive ability and more for his *patient capital*. Unlike many VCs who meddle heavily or chase rapid exits, Sacca's strategy was to back founders and wait, trusting compounding over control. His emotional restraint in letting ideas mature, even when tempted to optimise prematurely, led to outsized returns. Uber took years to prove viability. Twitter stumbled through multiple crises. Yet Sacca didn't flinch. His returns were not built on the perfect bet—but on *endurance through imperfection.*

Contrast these calm outperformers with figures whose wealth evaporated under emotional volatility. Consider the hedge funds that imploded in the aftermath of short-term bets gone wrong, or the amateur investors who built fortunes in crypto bubbles only to lose everything through overexposure, refusal to take measured profits, or panic exits. Their technical knowledge may have equalled or surpassed the calm outperformers, but their internal composition did not. They *reacted* instead of *responded.* Their financial engines were powerful, but their psychological brakes failed.

What's common across all these calm performers is not immunity from fear—it is their capacity to hold fear without obeying it. They establish systems that insulate them from their worst impulses. Buffett has his investment rules. Dalio has his principles. Blakely had her core product vision. Bogle had his low-cost mantra. These anchors aren't simply cognitive—they are *emotional boundaries.* They limit reactivity. They preserve direction. They create psychological compounding alongside financial compounding.

These individuals also curate environments that support steadiness. Buffett avoids fast-paced news cycles and rarely uses technology beyond basic tools. Bogle resisted the cult of personality that often surrounds financial gurus. Blakely built a company culture rooted in humour and long-term empowerment. Emotional discipline is not just internal willpower—it's also the *architecture around your choices.* Calm is easier when distraction is minimised, when support systems are in place, and when one's identity isn't tethered to constant validation.

One might assume this kind of steadiness is innate—a function of personality or upbringing. But many of these individuals actively trained it. Buffett studied behavioural economics before it was fashionable. Dalio used meditation to sharpen equanimity. Blakely practised reframing rejection as redirection. *Calm is a discipline*, not a default. It is built by rehearsing discomfort until discomfort no longer dictates action.

It's also worth noting that calm does not mean passive. These individuals acted boldly when conditions demanded it. Buffett's post-crisis investments were aggressive. Blakely took risks to launch with no retail backing. Dalio rebuilt a firm from near-zero. But these actions were *deliberate*, not *reactive*. They were chosen with clarity, not in panic. That distinction—between intentional risk-taking and emotional reactivity—is the subtle but vital hallmark of those who outperform consistently.

The calm outperformers don't just resist panic—they resist the compulsion to always optimise, always act, always intervene. They embrace what the Taoists call *wu wei*—the discipline of non-forcing. They understand that sometimes the most powerful move is *not to move*. They give strategies time to work. They give volatility space to settle. They understand that wealth is often a side effect of patience—not a reward for drama.

Their success invites a deeper question: how much of what we call "investment skill" is really just emotional regulation in disguise? Strip away jargon, analysis, and strategy, and the core habit remains: *stay centred under pressure*. Whether in markets, companies, or decisions, emotional composure is the multiplier on every other advantage. It preserves decision-making quality when stakes are highest. It extends time horizons when others shorten theirs. It sustains belief when feedback is scarce. It keeps compounding alive.

The lesson is clear: those who master calm do not avoid storms—they become unshakeable within them. Their edge is not noise, but nuance. Their wealth is not won in moments, but in their refusal to be moved by every moment. And if that is not the most transferable skill in finance—and in life—it is difficult to say what is.

Building Your Emotional Reserves

At the heart of every enduring financial strategy lies a less visible but more decisive asset: emotional capital. It is the capacity to remain rational in the presence of chaos, to sit with discomfort without reacting impulsively, to continue executing sound principles when they no longer feel rewarding in the short term. Yet while most personal finance literature focuses on accumulating monetary capital, far fewer resources address how to cultivate the *inner capacity* to withstand the emotional volatility that markets, careers, and even life itself inevitably impose. This gap is not trivial—it is foundational. Without emotional reserves, intellectual strategies collapse under pressure. Patience, discipline, and clear judgment are all downstream from the quality of one's emotional regulation.

Emotional capital is not fixed. It is not a trait we either inherit or lack. It is a *trainable resource*, like physical stamina or cognitive focus. And like those capacities, it must be developed through regular and intentional practice—often under non-ideal conditions. You do not grow calm in the absence of stress; you grow it by learning how to interpret, respond to, and ultimately reshape your reactions to stress. The cultivation of emotional capital is therefore an applied discipline. It integrates behavioural psychology, neuroplasticity, cognitive training, and practical mental models. It is not about eliminating emotion, but about learning to govern it with precision and self-awareness.

One of the most underappreciated training grounds for emotional capital is ordinary discomfort. Small frustrations—missed trains, awkward conversations, delayed outcomes—are daily invitations to rehearse non-reactivity. Every time you *notice the urge to react and instead pause*, you are building what psychologist Ethan Kross calls "psychological distance," the ability to observe thoughts and feelings without becoming submerged in them. This distancing isn't detachment in the cold or dismissive sense; rather, it is the capacity to remain *present without being hijacked.* In financial contexts, this might mean staying calm when a portfolio dips unexpectedly, or resisting the urge to reshuffle investments based on breaking news. It is the art of staying rooted in principle when your nervous system screams for action.

To build emotional reserves, you must first *identify the triggers that drain them.* For many, this means recognising cognitive biases—loss aversion, recency bias, or the illusion of control—that distort perception under stress. The investor who obsessively checks their portfolio multiple times a day is not merely managing data; they are attempting to manage anxiety through control. That act becomes counterproductive. Each check reinforces volatility salience and depletes composure. Instead, reframing your relationship to uncertainty is critical. A well-calibrated mind does not deny uncertainty—it expects it, accepts it, and plans for it.

Training this tolerance requires practice with delayed gratification. It's no coincidence that many elite performers—athletes, investors, or long-term thinkers—adopt routines that deliberately delay rewards. Fasting, cold exposure, endurance training, or long-form reading are not just hobbies; they are rituals of emotional training. These practices develop what neuroscientist Andrew Huberman refers to as "top-down control": the prefrontal cortex's ability to modulate limbic urges. When you consistently *choose structure over impulse*, you signal to the brain that discomfort is not danger—and over time, this rewires how you respond to uncertainty.

One of the most powerful tools for developing this circuitry is metacognition—the skill of thinking about your thinking. By naming your emotional states in real time ("I am feeling anxious because I just read a negative market headline"), you reduce their control over your behaviour. Labelling activates the prefrontal cortex, the region responsible for executive function, and dampens amygdala activity, which governs emotional reactivity. This mechanism has been well-documented in affective neuroscience and is a foundational practice in mindfulness-based stress reduction. In finance, this translates to greater clarity under volatility. The investor who can say "I feel the impulse to sell, but I also recognise this impulse as transient" will outperform the one who reacts without reflection—regardless of IQ.

Another overlooked contributor to emotional reserves is *identity structure*. People with fragile emotional capital often tie their self-worth too closely to outcomes. The entrepreneur who sees a failed product launch as a failed self, or the investor who views a market dip as personal incompetence, will burn emotional fuel quickly. To build emotional durability, you must anchor identity not to outcomes, but to processes. Ask not "Did I win today?" but "Did I act in alignment with my principles?" This subtle shift transforms every event—positive or negative—into feedback rather than judgment. Over time, this leads to greater composure, because self-worth no longer fluctuates with results. You are building the psychological equivalent of a fixed income portfolio: consistent, stable, and resilient.

Language, too, matters. The metaphors we use for stress shape how we experience it. Framing volatility as a test rather than a threat changes your neurophysiological response. This is not empty positivity—it is grounded in the work of cognitive behavioural therapy and appraisal theory. When you reframe discomfort as training, you metabolise it differently. The experience becomes energising rather than exhausting. Viktor Frankl's observation remains as potent today as when he wrote it: between stimulus and response, there is a space. In that space is your power to choose. And in that choice lies freedom, growth, and the slow accumulation of emotional wealth.

Mental models can also serve as stabilisers. The "inversion" model—popularised by Charlie Munger—asks you to examine your decisions by inverting the question: "What would I do if I wanted to sabotage myself financially?" When used regularly, this model makes emotional traps more visible. It externalises the stakes and reduces the chance of blind panic. Another powerful framework is the "barbell strategy" from Nassim Taleb: structure your life so that a small portion is exposed to high-risk, high-reward opportunities, while the majority remains ultra-conservative. This creates psychological safety while preserving optionality. Emotional reserves grow when decisions feel robust across possible futures.

Micro-habits compound here. Journaling, sleep, deep breathing, and strategic solitude all feed into your baseline regulation. These are not luxuries; they are infrastructure. A fatigued brain will default to short-termism. An overstimulated nervous system will seek immediate relief. Your capacity to withstand ambiguity is biologically tied to the quality of your recovery. As performance psychologist Jim Loehr has said, "Energy, not time, is the fundamental currency of high performance." Emotional energy is no exception.

It's important to note that emotional capital must be *diversified.* Composure in investing does not guarantee composure in relationships or health. These domains influence each other. A fragile home life or neglected body will eventually erode your financial decision-making. This is why elite performers often place enormous emphasis on rituals—daily walks, tech-free evenings, regular reflection. These are not indulgences; they are safeguards. They reduce cumulative volatility in other domains so that core performance remains steady.

And finally, emotional reserves are easier to sustain when values are clear. The investor driven only by numerical returns will eventually encounter a storm too irrational to weather. But the investor grounded in purpose—a desire to steward wealth for family, fund innovation, or model stewardship—will endure longer. Purpose lends perspective. It expands your time horizon. It lifts your tolerance for temporary pain. And that perspective—more than any spreadsheet, algorithm, or market edge—is what keeps you from flinching when the world goes mad.

Emotional capital is not earned once and held forever. It must be *renewed*, protected, and reinvested. Every choice you make—what you consume, how you respond, where you place attention—is a transaction. It either builds your reserves or depletes them. And over time, the balance in that emotional ledger will determine not only your wealth, but your ability to keep it.

Chapter 5
The Patience Flywheel: How Small Acts of Stillness Accelerate Over Time

Wealth rarely bursts onto the stage in a single dazzling moment. More often, it creeps into being—subtle, cumulative, born of countless small, unremarkable choices. This reality cuts against the grain of popular storytelling, which prefers the drama of jackpots, viral breakthroughs, or spectacular trades. Yet beneath the clamour of speculation lies a quieter machinery of prosperity: the patience flywheel. Borrowed from mechanical engineering, the flywheel does not gather speed from sudden force, but from steady repetition. It stores energy gradually, releasing it with remarkable persistence. In the economy of behaviour, patience is the axle on which this wheel turns. Tiny acts of restraint, repeated consistently, do not merely add up—they compound.

The great psychological snag is that patience rarely *feels* like advancement. It does not thrill the senses or provide instant validation. There are no flashing lights, no magazine covers. And yet, therein lies its strange potency. Its power is not visible at the point of action but accumulates silently across years, magnified by endurance. In wealth-building, stillness is not the same as stagnation; it is potential held in readiness. To grasp this is to unlearn much of what culture insists about progress.

We tend to misjudge where true leverage lies. Grand gestures and "big swings" are overvalued; humble micro-decisions are overlooked. Many chase the destination—riches—while neglecting the steadying process that sustains them. But compounding, whether of money, knowledge, or even temperament, thrives on rhythm. Financial independence is not a single leap but a refusal to interrupt the cadence of sound choices. The patience flywheel turns when you set an investment in motion and resist tinkering. It picks up speed when you endure volatility without flinching. It gains heft when you keep lifestyle inflation in check. It sharpens further when you train yourself to ignore noise. None of these moments inspire applause, but each adds torque to the wheel.

This chapter turns to the architecture of this hidden engine. Its central claim is simple yet provocative: in finance, as in life, the most remarkable outcomes often stem not from doing more, but from doing less—over longer spans. That premise cuts against instinct. Biologically, we are wired for immediacy, to respond and react. Externally, the world conspires to accelerate us—news tickers, alerts, "breaking" updates, every one of them a prod toward motion. The challenge, then, is not only intellectual but visceral. To remain still in such a climate is to swim upstream.

But stillness here should not be mistaken for passivity. It is intentional non-reactivity, the conscious decision to let time and compounding perform their quiet alchemy. Its feedback loops are slow, which is precisely why it feels unnatural. You may make an excellent decision and watch nothing change. Only maturity recognises that this absence of movement is not failure but the natural lag of compounding at work. The emotionally patient person does not lean on immediate feedback. Their compass is conviction, not confirmation.

So what, practically, drives the flywheel? Start with behaviour around money itself. The individual who automates savings and refuses to inflate their lifestyle at every pay rise is steadily loading the wheel with mass. Each month's discipline adds invisible momentum. What they build is not just a balance sheet but a stockpile of choices. Options, after all, are a form of wealth—psychological as much as financial. The knowledge that you *could* walk away makes you less likely to panic when others are twitching.

Now look at careers. The impatient professional jumps roles for modest increments; the patient one selects environments where compounding can occur—of skills, of networks, of trust. At first, nothing spectacular appears to happen. But depth matures into credibility, and credibility into autonomy—forms of capital that dwarf mere salary. Such arcs are not rapid, but when they bend, they bend decisively.

The investment realm provides perhaps the starkest contrast. The restless investor resets their compounding curve each time they chase a new fad. The disciplined counterpart, by holding steady, allows time itself to magnify returns beyond what any single clever allocation might achieve. It is not coincidental that many of history's most successful investors were those least inclined to check their portfolios. They understood that the enemy was not poor selection, but constant interference.

A paradox emerges: the less frantically you chase "more," the more you often achieve. This is not laziness but optimisation. Velocity seduces, but trajectory matters more. The impulsive actor, needing to undo past mistakes, seeks outsized wins. The patient counterpart requires no miracles; steady behaviour ensures they seldom fall into desperate circumstances at all.

There is also a diagnostic insight here. A hunger for sudden, life-changing victories often betrays an absence of consistent groundwork. When the flywheel has not been allowed to gather weight, one begins to hunt for levers. Yet levers introduce fragility. A single trade, a single company, a single gamble—yes, it can deliver brilliance. But it also courts devastation. Contrast that with the slow builder, whose diversification and steadiness create resilience. They are not hostage to a single outcome. Their ally is time itself.

The deeper gift of the flywheel is identity. Each act of patience confirms a belief about oneself: "I can remain disciplined when others cannot." That self-image becomes armour in volatile seasons. While peers ricochet between euphoria and despair, the patient actor stays aligned. Wealth, they know, is less about timing the market than about outlasting the crowd.

This chapter will trace those truths further—mapping how small decisions magnify over years, how patience fortifies not only finances but the psyche, and how optionality matures into freedom. It will argue for a shift of perspective: from chasing leverage in outcomes to embedding it in process; from demanding momentum to quietly compounding it; from craving visible proof to trusting invisible progress.

There are no shortcuts in this discipline, no dramatic reversals of fortune on offer. What exists is steady pressure—gentle, repetitive, relentless. Over time, that pressure shifts what once seemed immovable. The patient person does not merely wait. They accumulate. And in the end, they prevail—quietly, consistently, and without ever needing a spotlight.

The Mechanics of the Flywheel

If wealth creation were purely a matter of knowledge, spreadsheets would make millionaires of us all. But real wealth behaves less like a formula and more like a force—one powered not by brilliance or boldness, but by frictionless consistency over time. The patience flywheel captures this idea in full: that small, repeatable behaviours, if allowed to compound unimpeded, generate extraordinary momentum. Yet in practice, this is one of the least understood, most underutilised ideas in finance. It's not flashy. It doesn't promise speed. It promises durability.

A flywheel, in mechanical terms, is a rotating disc used to store energy. Once set in motion, it resists disruption and releases power gradually but reliably. It doesn't accelerate from a single push. It accelerates because you *keep pushing*—even when early spins feel slow, even when nothing seems to be happening. That's the metaphor. But unlike most metaphors in finance, this one is both literal and functional. Because when it comes to building enduring wealth, the most important moves are the ones so small you can barely see their impact—until time has had its say.

The power of the flywheel lies not in scale, but in continuity. A single act of financial restraint, in isolation, is negligible. Skipping one impulse purchase. Delaying one lifestyle upgrade. Sticking with one underwhelming but sound investment. None of these change your net worth overnight. But repeated over weeks, months, years? They become the scaffolding of optionality, liquidity, and compounding gains. *This is the patient person's leverage—the ability to do less, more often, with increasing effect.*

It helps to clarify that flywheel thinking is anti-fragile by design. Most people chase progress through intensity: cutting all expenses one month, splurging the next; jumping into a high-risk asset class, only to panic at the first downturn. Their emotional energy comes in spikes, their financial decisions in bursts. But the flywheel model doesn't rely on heroic effort. It is built on consistency that does not deplete. The inputs are simple: automated saving, reinvested dividends, learning done daily, not crammed reactively. These are not glamorous, but that's why they work. *They're too boring to burn out.*

To understand this more precisely, consider how time transforms effort. A person who saves £300 a month for 30 years at a modest return will almost always outperform someone who saves nothing for 29 years and then tries to make up for lost time with a large, late contribution. The latter requires far more capital and still yields less. The difference isn't intelligence or income. It's that the first person spun their flywheel early—and kept their hands off it. They understood that compounding is not a trick. It is a test of behavioural stamina.

This principle extends well beyond investments. In careers, the individual who consistently builds skills—whether through reading, networking, or disciplined craft—gains traction in the long term that no overnight pivot can replicate. Relationships, too, benefit from small, steady deposits of trust and attention. Even health—another domain riddled with short-term temptations—is governed by slow, repeated patterns. What emerges is a universal truth: *compounding rewards patience across domains, not because the activities themselves are dramatic, but because time makes them exponential.*

Yet there is an architectural genius in the flywheel most overlook: it is self-reinforcing. That is, *progress begets motivation.* The first six months of saving may feel thankless, but once a person sees evidence—a small but growing balance, the first dividend payment, the absence of stress from a sudden bill—momentum builds. Behaviour locks in. Patience feels purposeful. And with each act of reinforcement, emotional capital is also compounding. The flywheel isn't just storing financial energy. It's recalibrating self-identity. You stop thinking like a consumer and start behaving like an owner.

Of course, this requires a mindset shift. Most modern financial culture is fixated on leverage through shortcuts—through credit, risk, virality, or timing. The patience flywheel asks for the opposite: *leverage through process.* Through actions so dull, so unmarketable, they border on invisible. It's not about finding the next opportunity, but eliminating the need to. A person who has built enough emotional and financial velocity doesn't need perfect timing. They simply need to stay upright and in motion.

But here's the catch: the early stages feel unrewarding. The human brain, wired for stimulus and novelty, finds little dopamine in incrementalism. This is where many people fail—not because the process is difficult, but because the emotional reward system is misaligned with long-term outcomes. If the flywheel offers no praise, no visible spike in status or affirmation, people wrongly assume it's not working. *This is where discipline must exceed motivation.* That's not a popular message, but it is the accurate one.

There's also a deeper reason the flywheel works: it protects against behavioural decay. By automating good habits—financial and otherwise—you reduce reliance on willpower. You limit the number of decisions you need to make. And each time you remove choice from a good process, you reduce the chance of self-sabotage. The best investors automate contributions not just for convenience, but because it keeps their own psychology out of the way. In this context, the flywheel is not just a metaphor—it's a shield. It insulates against reactivity.

It's worth noting, too, that the patience flywheel plays a different game than the market. The market rewards stories and speculation in the short term. The flywheel rewards consistency and restraint in the long term. One is about performance; the other is about durability. They may occasionally overlap, but more often they don't. And in the end, it's the durable investor—not the dazzling one—who holds the advantage. The reason is simple: *process survives pressure.* Storytelling does not.

This is not a call to abandon ambition. It is a call to channel it differently. The most successful investors and entrepreneurs aren't devoid of urgency; they've simply redirected it. Their urgency is not in how quickly they can grow, but in how rigorously they protect consistency. They prioritise system over excitement. Process over prediction. And they know that their real edge is behavioural—not informational. The average person is searching for the next great opportunity. The flywheel thinker is searching for the next day they can stay on track.

By the time the flywheel is spinning, outcomes start to feel effortless. But this is deceptive. *What feels like ease is actually accumulated discipline.* And what feels like inevitable progress is just the by-product of thousands of good decisions—none of which were independently impressive. That's the paradox of the flywheel: the bigger it gets, the less it looks like work. But only because so much invisible work has gone into it.

Ultimately, the flywheel is a philosophy. It is a rejection of noise in favour of direction. It is a rebuttal to the idea that the fastest path is the most profitable. It is a belief—backed by behavioural science and real-world results—that the slow, the consistent, and the boring, when protected by patience, outperform the fast, the dramatic, and the reactive. Wealth doesn't shout. It whispers. And it whispers in the same rhythm as a flywheel gathering speed.

The Compounding of Small Decisions

One of the most underappreciated truths in the architecture of wealth is that outcomes are not driven by a handful of grand decisions, but by the quiet weight of thousands of small ones. These micro-decisions—how you allocate attention, spend £20, reply to a client, structure a morning routine—accumulate far more power than people assume. Their significance lies not in their immediate effect, but in their compounding trajectory. In isolation, they appear trivial; in sequence, they are transformative.

The financial world is fixated on the exceptional: the unicorn investment, the career breakthrough, the once-in-a-lifetime opportunity. But sustainable wealth has never depended on the extraordinary. It depends on consistency, and consistency is forged in small decisions. A monthly saving habit begun early, a series of modest but regular investments, a refusal to chase short-term returns—none of these stand out on their own. But over decades, they differentiate the financially resilient from the financially fragile.

Small decisions are not smaller versions of big ones—they are a different category of leverage altogether.

Consider this: choosing to invest £300 per month from the age of 25 rather than 35 doesn't just give you a ten-year head start. It gives you an exponential advantage because the returns on your earlier investments begin compounding *while* you're still making new ones. That decade of early compounding, often dismissed as negligible, is the difference between adequate savings and real financial freedom. It's not a matter of doing more. It's a matter of doing sooner—repeatedly.

In spending habits, the same principle holds. The decision to buy a slightly more expensive car, upgrade a phone more often, or dine out twice as frequently rarely feels consequential in the moment. But these decisions are not one-offs—they establish baselines. And baselines evolve into lifestyles. Once locked in, they create fixed costs that erode optionality. Emotional spending is often framed as a lack of control; more often, it's a failure to recognise the long-term cost of habituation. *What begins as a convenience becomes a commitment—and commitments have compounding effects too.*

Career trajectories are equally shaped by micro-decisions. Whether someone chooses to learn an adjacent skill, reach out to a mentor, or spend an extra thirty minutes refining their work doesn't feel like wealth-building at first glance. But these actions expand competence, reputation, and access over time. They alter career optionality not by leaps but by steady pivot. Individuals who build significant influence and autonomy rarely do so by a singular act. They do so through an accretion of decisions—most of which never appear in their biography.

The paradox of small decisions is that they are both easy to make and easy to ignore. They require little effort but also offer little immediate reward. This makes them psychologically difficult to prioritise. Human cognition tends to overweight the visible and the urgent. We are drawn to action that produces an immediate outcome. But real leverage lives in the invisible—the decision not to act impulsively, not to overreact, not to deviate from a long-term plan. *Discipline in the domain of the ordinary is the root of extraordinary results.*

Crucially, the compounding of small decisions depends on alignment, not perfection. You do not need to get every minor decision right. But you do need a framework that keeps your decisions pointing in the same direction. A clear investment philosophy, a deliberate approach to consumption, a repeatable method for evaluating risk—all these help convert sporadic decisions into a coherent process. And coherence is what allows compounding to remain uninterrupted. Every misaligned decision, by contrast, introduces friction. And friction is the enemy of momentum.

There is also a psychological dimension worth noting. The discipline required to make consistent small decisions builds not just financial capital but *identity capital.* Each act of restraint, foresight, or prudence reinforces the idea that you are someone who behaves with intent. Over time, this becomes a self-fulfilling cycle: identity drives behaviour, and behaviour confirms identity. This internal coherence is more stable than willpower. It's not about resisting temptation forever. It's about gradually becoming the kind of person who no longer finds the temptation interesting.

This concept becomes particularly relevant in environments of uncertainty. In volatile markets or career inflection points, people with a strong compounding mindset are less reactive because they've trained themselves to think in decades, not days. Their decisions are rarely dramatic because they don't need to be. They've built so much upstream alignment through years of thoughtful micro-decisions that the occasional shock doesn't destabilise them. *Resilience is not built during the storm—it's built in the stillness between storms.*

A common misconception is that the compounding effect of small decisions is linear. It is not. Like financial compounding, the returns are backloaded. The first few years may feel indistinguishable from stagnation. This is where most people give up, pivot, or self-sabotage. But for those who persist, the trajectory bends. Career visibility increases. Investments begin to yield disproportionately. Networks deepen. Insight accumulates. Eventually, the outcomes seem disconnected from the input. But they're not. They're the arithmetic of patience, hidden in plain sight.

This phenomenon mirrors what Jim Collins described as the "flywheel effect" in business. He observed that successful companies rarely pivoted on sudden breakthroughs. Instead, they pushed a heavy flywheel in the same direction, steadily, until momentum made the next push easier. This principle applies to individuals just as powerfully. You don't need dramatic reinvention. You need *directional persistence.* Each correct but unremarkable decision feeds the wheel. Each premature reversal slows it down.

Small decisions are not only scalable—they're survivable. In a world where risk is often glorified, this matters. Big, aggressive decisions may offer big returns, but they also carry big consequences. And most people are emotionally ill-equipped to absorb repeated shocks. The compounding mindset, by contrast, avoids unnecessary exposure. It optimises for *repeatability over rarity.* It builds an architecture of low-risk, high-frequency progress—progress that survives volatility and even benefits from it.

But sustaining this path requires clarity. You need to know what you're compounding toward. Without a long-term vision, even well-made small decisions become directionless. This is where frameworks like "identity-based investing," "second-order thinking," and "process over outcome" become vital. They convert intention into action and ensure that your compounding is not merely consistent but *coherent.* Otherwise, you risk perfect execution on an aimless trajectory.

The broader implication is this: wealth—financial or otherwise—is rarely won by talent, timing, or tactics alone. It is won by the cumulative power of seemingly insignificant decisions, made with care, aligned with purpose, and allowed to compound without interruption. The great differentiator is not access to information. It is the ability to stay with a good decision long enough for it to matter.

Ultimately, the real leverage of small decisions lies not in their magnitude but in their *repeatability.* They can be made daily, refined iteratively, and improved over time. They don't require a particular market cycle, network, or breakthrough moment. They only require presence, attention, and a deep respect for time. *Every day becomes an opportunity to compound intention into reality—not through force, but through patience applied consistently.* And in a world addicted to the illusion of overnight success, that remains the most enduring and underrated strategy of all.

The Role of Time in Exponential Growth

Time, unlike capital, cannot be borrowed, printed, or replaced. It moves with perfect consistency, unbending to will or emotion. And yet, it is routinely underestimated as a force in the shaping of wealth. While most financial advice fixates on returns—percentages, benchmarks, strategies—the deeper differentiator is how long those returns are allowed to compound. *Time is not a passive backdrop to growth; it is the multiplier that transforms restraint into results.*

The mathematics of exponential growth is widely known yet psychologically elusive. If someone offered you a penny doubled every day for thirty days, the offer would seem trivial at first—until you realised that it would exceed £5 million by the end. This is the structure of exponential compounding: slow, imperceptible beginnings followed by shockingly outsized outcomes. But in real life, people rarely give their decisions enough time to reach that exponential arc. They interrupt it, redirect it, or abandon it too early. *The problem is not that compounding doesn't work—it's that most people don't.*

What distinguishes the emotionally patient is not merely discipline—it is their relationship with time. They understand that time is not something to endure while waiting for results; it is the engine that *creates* those results. Emotionally reactive investors often fixate on the next quarter. Emotionally resilient ones think in quarters of centuries. This isn't just a preference for long-termism; it's a practical recognition that value creation occurs when time is allowed to magnify small advantages into structural ones.

Consider Warren Buffett. He is often praised for his investment acumen, but the more telling detail is that over 95% of his net worth came after his 65th birthday. His returns, while impressive, were not anomalously high; what was anomalous was how long he maintained them uninterrupted. The real lesson is not how to earn 20% returns—it's how to stay invested long enough for those returns to matter. *Time rewards those who remove themselves from the tyranny of immediate feedback.*

The mechanics of exponential growth demand emotional patience precisely because progress is not linear. The early stages are thankless. You invest, save, or build without visible payoff. This period is where most people quit—not because they're lazy, but because the feedback loop is misaligned with their expectations. They've been conditioned to expect progress in proportion to effort. But compounding is indifferent to early effort; it rewards duration, not drama. And this creates a psychological threshold that only a few are trained to cross.

In behavioural finance, this is reflected in what's known as "time inconsistency"—the tendency to value immediate rewards disproportionately compared to future ones. When asked to choose between £100 today and £110 in a month, many people choose the former. But if the choice is between £100 in a year and £110 in thirteen months, they choose the latter. The difference is negligible financially, but psychologically it exposes our bias. We discount future rewards not because they're small, but because they're distant. *Emotional capital, then, is the ability to bridge that distance without self-sabotage.*

In the context of wealth, this time sensitivity explains why so few investors hold through downturns. The value of time is greatest precisely when the emotional cost of patience is highest. Market corrections, career stagnation, business plateaus—all of these are invitations to abandon course. But abandoning early converts exponential curves into flat lines. It resets progress at the very moment the compounding starts to accelerate. This is not just a loss of opportunity—it is a *systemic error in reasoning* about time.

The same pattern applies in non-financial domains. Skills, relationships, reputations—none of them grow linearly. You don't become respected by delivering one excellent result. You become respected by *repeatedly* delivering quality, often unrecognised, until the credibility curve inflects. That inflection doesn't happen with effort alone. It happens with effort over time. And the irony is that people often quit just before the compounding effect begins to accelerate. Not because they lack the ability, but because they cannot emotionally justify the wait.

What magnifies this further is how exponential growth feeds back into itself. As results begin to compound, they create a reinforcing loop of confidence, capability, and optionality. Confidence leads to better decisions. Capability attracts better opportunities. Optionality protects against bad outcomes. Over decades, this becomes structural advantage—not because of any single decision, but because of *uninterrupted coherence across time.* Those who can stay the course unlock not just greater outcomes but more resilient foundations.

This also reframes how we should think about risk. Conventional wisdom views risk as volatility—price movements, uncertainty, variance. But for the emotionally patient, the greatest risk is *interrupting compounding.* Selling too early, pivoting too often, switching too frequently—these are not cautious acts; they are erosive ones. The longer one can stay directionally aligned, the more forgiving the path becomes. Time neutralises volatility but punishes inconsistency. *The emotional cost of staying the course is high—but the mathematical cost of not doing so is higher still.*

A second-order insight here is that patience is not passive. It's not about sitting idle or tolerating mediocrity. It is *active endurance*—a deliberate choice to prioritise coherence over stimulation, longevity over novelty. It requires mental models that reinforce conviction: second-order thinking, inversion, probabilistic reasoning, and above all, *a philosophy of compounding.* Without a philosophy, time feels empty. With it, time becomes an asset class in itself.

This helps explain why emotional steadiness is such a rare financial advantage. It's not because the concept is complex—it's because the practice is psychologically counterintuitive. We live in an optimisation culture obsessed with velocity: how fast can we grow, scale, monetise? But the most durable forms of wealth compound *quietly*, not quickly. They resist the need to constantly prove their value because they are grounded in long horizons. And the more you align with that horizon, the less tempted you are to chase temporary gains.

Real wealth, then, is time made visible. It is not measured by possessions, but by the optionality and freedom that accumulated compounding affords. And that compounding isn't merely financial—it is cognitive, relational, emotional. Someone who understands the role of time makes different choices not because they are more rational, but because they are more grounded. They trade urgency for inevitability. They play a game that others don't even see being played.

That is the true leverage of exponential growth: it converts emotional restraint into strategic advantage. It allows the patient to outperform not by trying harder, but by *interrupting themselves less.* They understand that exponential outcomes are not driven by extraordinary acts. They are driven by *ordinary acts, sustained extraordinarily long.* And while that may not satisfy the ego in the short term, it decisively compounds in the long term—if, and only if, you give it the one thing it cannot generate for itself: *time.*

Escaping the Need for Big Wins

The obsession with breakthrough success—lottery jackpots, overnight unicorns, ten-bagger stocks—is not merely a by-product of greed; it is often a symptom of emotional depletion. When people lack the inner endurance to wait, they seek ways to leap. When their emotional capital is thin, their tolerance for slow returns collapses, and the allure of high-risk shortcuts becomes irresistible. *But emotionally resilient individuals understand a different law: real wealth is not seized—it is steadily permitted to accumulate.*

The psychology of needing a big win is often disguised as ambition. But beneath the surface, it is typically rooted in discomfort with uncertainty and impatience with gradual progress. The promise of a dramatic payout offers not just money, but psychological relief: a quick resolution to the discomfort of waiting. In markets, this manifests in speculative investing; in careers, it manifests in burnout from chasing promotion after promotion; in entrepreneurship, it shows up as premature scaling or pivoting without traction. What these behaviours share is an underlying intolerance for the slow, invisible, compounding work that actually builds lasting value.

Emotionally steady individuals are not immune to ambition—they simply *refuse to stake their future on statistical outliers*. They internalise the asymmetric danger of chasing improbable wins: if your financial plan depends on something extraordinary happening, then by definition, your plan is extraordinarily fragile. Instead of hoping for upside surprises, they build systems that expect nothing exceptional and still deliver strong outcomes. This orientation is not born of caution, but of sophistication. It is the product of understanding that risk-adjusted returns are not about *maximum growth*, but *maximum durability*.

There is a quiet power in refusing to be dazzled by hype. Consider the contrast between two archetypes: the person who trades aggressively, seeking to double their money in a year, versus the one who invests in diversified assets and waits a decade. The former may occasionally win big—but the latter almost always wins consistently. The key difference is not intelligence, but *time horizon and emotional posture*. Emotionally grounded people know that volatility is not a test of intellect, but of temperament. And they build lives that don't rely on perfect timing or rare luck.

This mindset shows up clearly in the way resilient people make career decisions. They aren't seduced by every new opportunity with a bigger title or slightly higher pay. They prioritise *trajectory over theatrics*—seeking roles that offer compounding learning, exposure to thoughtful people, and reputational endurance. They understand that the best careers are rarely the result of a single bold move, but of hundreds of small, reputation-building decisions made over years. They also understand that the cost of a misstep is not just financial—it can be psychic. Big wins that blow up extract more than money; they drain confidence, burn social capital, and derail momentum.

In investing, the most dangerous myth is that one needs to "get in early" or "find the next big thing." This has bred entire generations of people who equate financial success with early access—whether to hot IPOs, crypto, or venture deals. But this overlooks the far more powerful truth: *you don't need a big win if you remove the need for one*. By reducing lifestyle inflation, cultivating multiple income streams, and maintaining liquidity buffers, emotionally resilient people build portfolios—and lives—that don't require heroics to work. Their success becomes inevitable, not because of any one decision, but because of *how few decisions must go right.*

The best investors are not those who chase the highest returns—they're those who avoid fatal mistakes. When you observe long-term outperformers, the pattern is not aggressive betting but consistent restraint. They spend less time swinging for the fences and more time avoiding unforced errors. And over long time horizons, *not losing becomes the dominant strategy for winning.* Emotional resilience thus becomes a kind of competitive edge—not because it produces fireworks, but because it keeps the engine running through quiet seasons.

This restraint is not passive. It requires cognitive discipline. The emotionally resilient person must regularly resist the temptation to tinker, over-optimise, or abandon a plan prematurely. They cultivate what some behavioural economists call "strategic inertia"—the ability to stick with well-thought-out systems even when results are not immediately flattering. They trust the architecture of their decisions more than the mood of the moment. And this trust is earned—not from blind faith, but from *knowing how compounding actually works.*

The market punishes impatience precisely because most people have it. Asset prices surge when narratives take over. But those narratives often rest on assumptions that are flimsy and short-lived. Emotionally impulsive investors get swept up in these waves. Resilient ones anchor themselves in fundamentals—not just economic, but personal. They ask not only "What might this asset return?" but "Can I sleep at night while owning it?" and "Will this choice still make sense to me in five years?" This is the essence of financial maturity: being able to *calibrate your decisions to your nervous system.*

Big wins have another hidden cost: they distort expectations. Once someone experiences a windfall, it becomes the new benchmark. Everything slower starts to feel like failure. This is why lottery winners, professional athletes, and some tech founders struggle with burnout, anxiety, or poor financial decisions post-success. The psychology of maintenance is radically different from the psychology of attainment. Emotionally resilient individuals train for the long game. They don't let success destabilise them because their identity isn't tied to outcomes—it's grounded in principles, routines, and systems that don't require adrenaline to function.

There's also a moral dimension here. Escaping the need for big wins enables people to act more ethically. When survival or perceived success depends on a massive outcome, it becomes easier to justify questionable tactics—cutting corners, misleading others, or taking on hidden risks. But when your strategy is built on steady accumulation and low downside exposure, you're freed from that moral hazard. You can afford to be honest, patient, and even generous—because your wealth doesn't depend on short-term victory, but long-term validity.

That is the paradox: playing a smaller game often produces larger results. Not because the targets are lower, but because the emotional system behind them is sturdier. A resilient strategy doesn't aim to be thrilling. It aims to be enduring. It tolerates boredom, volatility, and ambiguity not because it enjoys them, but because it knows what they lead to. Over time, the advantages of this approach compound—not just financially, but psychologically. Life becomes calmer, decisions clearer, and outcomes more robust.

To build a life that doesn't need big wins is not to settle—it is to *elevate your threshold for panic.* It is to structure your goals, habits, and finances in a way that insulates you from the randomness of the world. It is to prioritise the *slow burn of progress* over the quick flash of excitement. And it is to understand that real leverage comes not from risking more, but from needing less.

This is not a message of limitation. It is one of liberation. When you no longer require the extraordinary, you can focus on the sustainable. When you no longer chase the improbable, you can master the inevitable. And when you stop needing the next big win, *you free yourself to play a game that is quietly but decisively yours to win.*

Chapter 6
Volatility Tolerance: Making Peace with Uncertainty

Modern life hides a peculiar illusion: that uncertainty is a glitch to be fixed, an inconvenience we'll soon engineer out of existence. We design portfolios as though volatility were an anomaly rather than the essence of markets. We draft neat career plans as if the years would unfold obediently, undisturbed by the jaggedness of reality. And when shocks arrive—political upheaval, market crashes, unexpected turns in our own lives—we often respond not only with alarm but with indignation, as though the universe had broken its contract of predictability. Yet the harder truth is this: uncertainty is not an exception but the rule, not a bug but the fabric itself. And mastery lies not in eliminating it but in operating with composure within its grip.

Volatility tolerance is too easily reduced to the idea of "bearing losses." It is more than that. It is the art of holding direction when the map dissolves, of refusing to hand your emotional balance over to chaos. It is not achieved by consuming another economic outlook or predictive chart, but by retraining the nervous system to resist the reflex to flinch. Some of the most enduring fortunes—financial or otherwise—owe less to clairvoyance than to the simple ability to stay rational while storms raged. Those who metabolise uncertainty, rather than flee from it, gain an uncommon edge: durability.

Markets, naturally, provide the clearest demonstration. Prices move not on pristine information but on the churn of fear, hope, and randomness colliding in real time. The volatility is not distortion around the signal—it *is* the signal. If your clarity depends on calm seas, you will never leave the harbour. But train yourself for turbulence—expect it, rehearse for it, detach action from anxiety—and volatility transforms from threat into opportunity. Fragile actors are punished. The prepared are enriched.

This doesn't mean recklessness. Tolerating volatility is not about blunting fear, but about refining calibration so that stress does not automatically provoke reaction. The emotionally resilient are not devoid of apprehension; they are simply slower to be thrown off course. That steadiness is the result of philosophy, deliberate conditioning, and accumulated exposure. They have discovered that many apparent threats are merely unfamiliar sensations. Like a muscle, tolerance grows not by avoiding strain but by increasing load in increments and holding form under it.

A conceptual shift is required. Stop asking how to erase uncertainty; ask how to function intelligently within it. Every domain—markets, careers, relationships, even health—runs on probability, not guarantees. Yet many of our worst errors stem from the fantasy of certainty. When expectations are violated, panic ensues—not because reality betrayed us, but because we failed to expect its ambiguity. To demand certainty of a probabilistic world is not just naïve. It is perilous. Fragility, the inevitable by-product, is ruinously expensive in compounding systems.

Here, Nassim Nicholas Taleb's notion of anti-fragility sharpens the lens. Robustness resists shocks; anti-fragility grows from them. Muscles repair stronger after strain, immune systems calibrate through exposure, markets reprice efficiently after corrections. The aim, then, is not insulation from volatility but alignment with it—building habits, structures, and mindsets that profit from disturbance. Redundancy, optionality, and calm under pressure form the toolkit. This is not about swinging for jackpots. It is about ensuring survival long enough to let chaos pay dividends.

Once volatility is reframed, its signals multiply. Risk and opportunity often share the same face, depending on the emotional posture of the observer. A plunging stock may be panic's waste—or value's invitation. A jittery job market may hide not collapse but fluidity, creating fresh openings. A global crisis may destabilise today yet seed innovation tomorrow. The reactive mind contracts under uncertainty. The resilient one leans in, asking: "What is being revealed here that others, blinded by fear, will miss?"

This tolerance also carries a subtler virtue: humility. When we accept the limits of foresight, we shift focus from prediction to process. Paradoxically, this produces stronger outcomes. We begin designing for survival, not luck. We favour positions with limited downside and asymmetric upside. We stop wagering on everything going right. The fixation on the next clever move gives way to refining the framework guiding *all* moves.

And here is the crucial insight: you do not rise to your expectations; you fall to your training. Volatility tolerance is not abstract. It is embodied. It is trained. It is rehearsed through countless small exposures—taking modest stakes in uncertain environments, deciding without perfect clarity, practising calm speech under pressure. These are the micro-reps. Waiting until crisis strikes to build resilience is folly. Those with true emotional wealth prepare in advance, training for turbulence before the skies darken.

The same lesson scales upward. Elite organisations—hedge funds, special forces, high-performing start-ups—spend less energy on seeking certainty than on rehearsing for chaos. They run simulations, post-mortems, contrarian stress-tests. Their question is not "How do we prevent disorder?" but "How do we behave when it arrives?" This institutional conditioning makes calm action possible when rivals freeze. At the individual level, practices like pre-defined exit strategies, diversified time horizons, and regular reviews serve the same purpose: emotional shock absorbers built in advance.

The broader implication is inescapable. Volatility is not a design flaw; it is the entrance fee for meaningful growth. Emotional wealth begins not with silencing uncertainty, but with engineering oneself to stay upright within it. It marks a pivot from seeking comfort to cultivating competence. From fighting the unknown to folding it into strategy.

This chapter tracks that pivot. It dismantles the myth of predictability, then lays out frameworks for recasting risk as information. Along the way, you will encounter thinkers such as Taleb, practitioners who deliberately train in ambiguity, and investors who treat volatility as the toll for accessing long-term upside. Practical tools for building tolerance—controlled exposure, cognitive reframing, disciplined systems—will be placed in your hands.

Nothing here is abstract. Each principle has consequences for your portfolio, your work, your resilience. What emerges is a sturdier core and a clearer lens. And perhaps, most critically, the recognition that wealth is less about perfect answers than about adaptive composure. That calm amid the unknowable—not clairvoyance—is the truest hedge against uncertainty.

The Inescapability of Uncertainty

It is an error both subtle and widespread to treat uncertainty as a temporary inconvenience—something to be minimised, hedged, or ultimately conquered with enough data, planning, or intelligence. This attitude is deeply embedded in the architecture of modern life: we pursue predictive models, obsess over metrics, and idolise the illusion of control. But underneath this collective choreography lies a more discomforting truth: *uncertainty is not a transient flaw in the system—it is the system's default state.* It cannot be eliminated; it can only be navigated. And this realisation is not defeatist—it is liberating.

To approach uncertainty as a condition to be solved is to invite chronic dissatisfaction. It leads to rigid strategies, brittle expectations, and a recurring sense of betrayal when events refuse to unfold as planned. This mindset misinterprets the nature of both markets and life. Financial markets are not puzzles with a final answer—they are dynamic ecosystems shaped by feedback loops, behavioural biases, regulatory shifts, and random shocks. Life decisions—career arcs, relationships, even personal health—follow similarly complex trajectories. Outcomes depend not only on effort or skill but on timing, path-dependence, and externalities that no amount of forecasting can fully capture.

The paradox is that the more we try to deny uncertainty, the more vulnerable we become to it. We build elaborate models with misleading precision. We overcommit to narratives that match our worldview. We confuse clarity with certainty. And then, when reality refuses to cooperate—when markets crash, companies fail, or life takes an unplanned turn—we interpret it not as part of the design, but as a breakdown. *But it is not a breakdown. It is business as usual.* To thrive in such an environment requires not the eradication of uncertainty but a reorientation of our psychological and strategic relationship to it.

This is especially true in the realm of investing. Many people approach markets with a subconscious desire for control: "If I read enough, if I study hard enough, I'll beat the system." But markets are not problems that yield to diligence alone. They are arenas of probabilistic outcomes, where even the best analyses can be undone by sentiment, liquidity shocks, or global events beyond comprehension. The most successful investors are not those who predict the future accurately—they are those who *construct portfolios that function despite the future being unknowable.* They embrace uncertainty not as a gap in knowledge but as a central operating principle. That distinction changes everything.

Ray Dalio, founder of Bridgewater Associates, famously built his investment philosophy around the idea that he could be wrong. He created systems that stress-tested ideas against multiple scenarios and dissenting views. Warren Buffett repeatedly highlights that the key to his success is not genius-level foresight but *an insistence on a margin of safety*—a structural buffer against being wrong. These practitioners do not see uncertainty as a bug to be fixed, but as the basis for robust decision-making. *The durability of their strategies comes not from eliminating risk, but from integrating it.*

Outside markets, the same principle holds. In careers, most trajectories are not linear but characterised by abrupt shifts—technological disruptions, corporate restructurings, personal reinventions. The assumption that careers should proceed smoothly from one milestone to the next is not only false—it sets people up to feel like failures for experiencing what is, in truth, normal volatility. Those who succeed over time tend to be less fixated on avoiding detours and more focused on *retaining optionality and learning capacity throughout them.* They understand that uncertainty is not just a barrier—it is a signal-rich environment for adaptation.

The psychological resistance to uncertainty is understandable. Human brains are wired to prefer predictability; we evolved to associate ambiguity with danger. But modern uncertainty is rarely life-threatening. It is cognitive and emotional—it produces anxiety, indecision, and status fear. The challenge, then, is not to eradicate uncertainty from the environment, but to *expand our nervous system's ability to remain functional within it.* This is what separates emotional endurance from mere optimism. Optimism hopes things will improve. Emotional endurance operates even when they don't.

A key turning point for most people is the shift from seeking control to seeking *clarity of posture.* This means accepting that the inputs cannot always be managed, but the outputs—your decisions, your response, your stance—can. Uncertainty ceases to be paralysing when you adopt a systems-level view. Rather than trying to predict exactly which bet will succeed, you focus on *designing a set of bets that are collectively resilient.* Rather than waiting for the perfect opportunity, you develop *principled heuristics for action in imperfect situations.* These are not backup plans—they are primary strategies for living in an inherently unstable world.

Much of modern productivity culture, ironically, reinforces the wrong relationship to uncertainty. It implies that with enough habits, hacks, and hacks-for-your-habits, life can be wrestled into predictability. But real leverage comes from learning to work effectively *through fog, not just in sunshine.* A leader who can make decisions with 60% of the data and revise them as new evidence emerges is far more powerful than one who waits for full clarity. An investor who maintains a consistent process through drawdowns is more likely to outperform one who overreacts to every new data point. Emotional resilience begins with the understanding that *operating amid uncertainty is a core skill, not a temporary condition to endure.*

There is also a subtle ethical dimension to how we handle uncertainty. People who believe the world should be more predictable than it is are more prone to blame, both self-directed and external. They interpret setbacks as moral failings—"I should have known better"—rather than as probabilistic outcomes. But a mature relationship with uncertainty includes *grace.* It acknowledges that good decisions can lead to bad outcomes and vice versa. It separates process from outcome in a way that maintains learning without collapsing into shame or self-deception. This orientation makes us not only more effective, but more humane—toward ourselves and others.

Normalising uncertainty also invites a broader humility in our models of progress. When we let go of linearity as the default narrative, we open space for exploration, for non-traditional metrics of success, for meaningful detours. Careers do not have to escalate in a straight line. Investments do not have to outperform every quarter. Personal growth does not have to follow an annual performance review structure. What matters is *trajectory over time, not immediate legibility*. Uncertainty, when accepted, allows us to play the long game without burning out on the short one.

This brings us to an even deeper insight: *uncertainty is not merely something to cope with—it is the environment in which original thought, outsized returns, and meaningful breakthroughs emerge.* If everything were predictable, nothing would be mispriced. If every step were mapped, no innovation would be needed. Uncertainty is the friction that makes skill relevant. It is the condition that forces adaptive learning. And it is the backdrop against which emotional wealth—the ability to function, decide, and build amid chaos—becomes the rarest asset of all.

Thus, the goal is not serenity through avoidance, but strength through exposure. Just as physical training involves controlled stress, emotional and strategic resilience grows through consistent contact with the unknown. This article—and the chapter it anchors—is not about inoculating you against risk, but about giving you the philosophical and practical scaffolding to live well within its bounds. To stop waiting for the world to settle, and instead start operating as if *volatility were the default setting of reality*—because it is.

This change in posture—toward uncertainty as a *condition to design for rather than a problem to solve*—is subtle but profound. It will not make the world more stable. But it will make you less brittle. And that, in a compounding world, is a decisive advantage.

Reframing Risk as Opportunity

Most people misread risk because they misunderstand volatility. To the untrained eye, market swings, career instability, or geopolitical flux signal danger—something to flee or hedge at all costs. But to the strategically aware, these same movements represent *potential.* Risk, properly understood, is not the enemy of stability—it is the price of asymmetry. Volatility, when framed correctly, becomes not a threat but a portal: an entry point for those equipped with patience, perspective, and preparation.

The core mistake is conflating volatility with loss. They are not synonymous. Volatility is movement—up, down, or sideways. Loss is a realised negative outcome. The former is a condition; the latter is a result. When volatility is interpreted purely as instability, the reflex is withdrawal—sell off assets, delay action, seek refuge in certainty. But this instinct locks people out of value precisely when it becomes available. *The premium for taking risk exists because most people flee when it shows up.* The few who can remain clear-headed in its presence are rewarded disproportionately.

Consider a fundamental truth of markets: *the best prices do not appear in calm conditions.* They emerge amid fear, disorder, and dislocation. The 2008 financial crisis punished those over-leveraged or short-sighted, but it created generational wealth for those who held dry powder and emotional discipline. Airbnb, Uber, and WhatsApp were all born between 2007 and 2009. These were not anomalies. They were the upside of dislocation. To participate in such upside, one must first decouple discomfort from dysfunction. Volatility may feel destabilising, but it often *creates the inefficiencies that allow rational actors to outperform.*

The same holds in careers. The highest-return moves often come from transitions—moments when industries are shifting, roles are being redefined, or companies are willing to take unconventional bets. These transitions feel risky because they lack precedent. But they *present opportunity precisely because most people are hesitant to act within them.* The future is rarely divided evenly among the prepared and unprepared; it is divided among those who can tolerate temporary ambiguity versus those who can't.

To reframe risk as opportunity is not to romanticise chaos. It is to shift from a defensive psychology—"How do I protect myself?"—to a constructive one—"Where is the inefficiency I can absorb, the asymmetry I can engage?" This posture does not require recklessness. On the contrary, it demands structure. When risk is seen as the cost of meaningful upside, the goal becomes *not avoidance but optimisation*. What can be controlled is the exposure, the context, the time horizon—not the presence of risk itself. *Risk cannot be eliminated; it can only be chosen wisely.*

One of the most powerful tools for reframing risk is the concept of *optional asymmetry*. In most valuable pursuits, the downside is capped—limited to time, money, or short-term status. But the upside, if realised, is disproportionately large. Writing a book, starting a business, learning a new skill, investing in an unpopular sector—each appears risky because success is uncertain. But the asymmetry lies in the payoff: the most you can lose is often knowable and finite; the most you can gain is unknown and open-ended. *The wise embrace of such optionality is a defining trait of resilient wealth builders.*

It is not a coincidence that many of history's most successful investors—Howard Marks, Charlie Munger, Peter Lynch—speak of risk not as a numerical abstraction but as a behavioural edge. What they share is not merely analytical skill, but a calibrated comfort with ambiguity. They do not seek to eliminate risk from their portfolios; they *design portfolios that require risk to generate excess return*. They invest in situations where the consensus has priced fear, but not properly calibrated the long-term reward.

This behavioural edge extends beyond capital markets. Entrepreneurs who create enduring businesses are not gamblers—they are engineers of upside. They study where others see chaos, build when others retreat, and iterate through failure. Their secret is not fearlessness—it is clarity: they understand that *risk is the gatekeeper of outsized return*. To bypass it is to forfeit the path entirely.

Importantly, reframing risk requires a shift in time horizon. Most fears are born of short-term thinking. Volatility seems intolerable when viewed through the lens of weeks or months. But stretched over years or decades, its role transforms. *Volatility is not noise; it is the mechanism through which value gets transferred from the impatient to the patient.* This insight recasts the emotional experience of downturns. A drop in asset value is not an indictment of the strategy—it may be the setup for future gain. The question is not whether volatility will occur—it is whether your system and temperament are designed to benefit from it.

This reframing also reveals the hidden cost of safety. Playing it safe—parking wealth in cash, staying in a secure job, clinging to consensus views—feels responsible. But it often results in the slow erosion of potential. Inflation compounds. Industries evolve. Opportunities expire. *Risk aversion is not free—it quietly charges interest in the form of missed growth, stagnant learning, and strategic fragility.* The illusion of safety often masks the inevitability of decline.

A more adaptive approach is to *differentiate between visible risk and actual risk*. Much of what appears risky—market corrections, career pivots, starting small—is simply *visible volatility*. But true risk is *irreversibility without reward*—betting everything on one outcome, lacking redundancy, becoming psychologically brittle in uncertainty. These are the dangers worth avoiding. Not the fluctuations, but the traps.

Reframing risk also allows for better communication—internally and with others. Leaders who treat risk as taboo foster environments of conformity. But those who model intelligent engagement with uncertainty create space for initiative, experimentation, and resilience. In investing, in strategy, and in personal development, this clarity becomes contagious. People do not need protection from risk—they need language and frameworks to interact with it constructively.

Cognitively, one of the most powerful tools for this reframe is *probabilistic thinking*. When we stop asking "Will this succeed?" and start asking "What is the range of outcomes, and what am I exposed to in each?" we regain agency. Probabilities shift the emotional burden from binary success/failure into a continuum of outcomes. They allow for better calibration, better de-risking, and more grounded confidence. *Not in the certainty of outcome, but in the integrity of process.*

The emotional corollary is *self-distancing*. Many people overreact to risk because they interpret outcomes as reflections of their identity. But when risk is framed as external—when decisions are depersonalised and understood as experiments within a broader system—emotional clarity improves. This does not dull ambition; it strengthens execution. It allows one to make bolder moves without self-immolation if they don't work out.

Ultimately, reframing risk as opportunity is a moral decision as much as a strategic one. It is a vote of confidence in learning over fear, in compounding over protectionism, in initiative over stasis. It acknowledges that the world is not designed to be predictable—but that meaning and mastery emerge when we engage it anyway. To live wisely is not to sidestep risk. It is to *design a life and strategy that converts risk into relevance.* That shift—from avoidance to engagement—is the origin of leverage in a volatile world.

The Anti-Fragility Advantage

Most systems are either robust or fragile. When stress is applied to the fragile, they shatter. When pressure meets the robust, they endure—but nothing improves. Then there is a rare third category, first rigorously articulated by Nassim Nicholas Taleb: systems that *benefit from disorder.* These are not merely resilient; they are *anti-fragile.* Volatility, randomness, and shock do not just test them—they *strengthen* them. In a world that is neither stable nor predictable, anti-fragility may be the single most important conceptual advantage in wealth, life, and strategy.

The concept is deceptively simple: what gains from uncertainty has an edge that fragile systems never will. The anti-fragile does not merely recover from disruption—it *requires* it. Biological evolution, free markets, entrepreneurial innovation, and even wisdom itself depend on stressors. Without challenge, they atrophy. With challenge, they adapt. Taleb's formulation draws a line between what survives and what *thrives* in chaos. Most people—and most investment philosophies—are built to avoid chaos. The anti-fragile operator, by contrast, *designs around it,* knowing that real gains are buried in unpredictability.

The financial implications are profound. Fragile portfolios rely on stability—on the assumption that tomorrow will look like yesterday. When that assumption fails, so do they. Anti-fragile portfolios, however, are constructed with optionality. They are exposed to unlimited upside and limited downside. A classic example is the barbell strategy: place the majority of capital in ultra-safe assets, and a small percentage in extremely high-risk, high-reward options. This configuration benefits from the unexpected—because when volatility spikes, the optionality pays off, while the base remains intact. *It is not about prediction. It is about structure.*

Anti-fragility also explains why some individuals repeatedly rise stronger after crisis. They don't just bounce back—they *emerge more capable.* This isn't resilience in the conventional sense. Resilience implies restoration of the prior state. Anti-fragility means *transformation* to a stronger one. Entrepreneurs who iterate through failure, investors who recalibrate in downturns, professionals who reinvent themselves under pressure—these are not just persistent. They are structurally adaptive. They have configured their work, habits, and psychology not just to absorb shocks, but to be *improved by them.*

This is not merely theoretical. Consider Amazon. Its sprawling infrastructure was originally derided as wasteful, but became a strategic moat when global logistics fractured during the COVID-19 pandemic. Or take the venture capital model: most startups fail, but the structure of VC portfolios—massive asymmetric upside concentrated in a few firms—ensures that volatility is not just tolerable, but essential. The very nature of these models *requires noise, surprise, and deviation* to generate value. Stability would actually reduce their returns.

On a personal level, anti-fragility shows up in routines that inject manageable stress. Physical training, when calibrated properly, creates stronger muscles by tearing fibres. Intermittent fasting, intellectual debate, and even emotional hardship—if framed and integrated correctly—can increase capacity. What matters is not the avoidance of pain, but *the ability to integrate challenge in ways that multiply capability.* This is a worldview shift: from protecting one's current state to *designing systems that extract utility from shock.*

This lens also explains why so many legacy institutions and risk-averse individuals falter in modern markets. They seek to *smooth volatility*, eliminate surprises, and over-optimise for efficiency. But over-optimisation breeds fragility. Just-in-time supply chains work perfectly—until one node fails. Leveraged bets generate spectacular returns—until liquidity dries up. The anti-fragile thinker avoids such brittleness by *leaving slack in the system*. They avoid maximising for the short term in favour of longer-term adaptability.

Another essential feature of anti-fragility is *redundancy*. At first glance, redundancy looks inefficient—extra resources, idle capacity, unallocated cash. But in a stochastic world, redundancy is not waste; it is *resilience converted into strategic advantage*. It allows for optionality, for tactical flexibility, for shock absorption. People with emotional redundancy—those who are not chronically overcommitted or reactive—respond to stress by making better decisions. They are not maxed out. They have *room to manoeuvre* when others panic.

Crucially, anti-fragility is not a personality trait—it is a *design principle*. It can be embedded in how you manage time, deploy capital, craft agreements, or select career paths. It rewards decentralisation, modular thinking, and asymmetry. Its ethics are not based on controlling the future, but on making yourself *positionally advantaged* when the future deviates from expectations. This is not easy. It requires humility—an acceptance that prediction is fragile, that models fail, that the world punishes overconfidence. But the reward is extraordinary: *you stop fearing change because change becomes your fuel.*

The concept also demands a reframing of failure. In a fragile system, failure is fatal. In an anti-fragile system, failure is *data*. Not all failure is constructive, of course. But when contained, analysed, and iterated upon, it feeds the broader system. This is why anti-fragile strategies prioritise experimentation—small bets, frequent feedback loops, reversible decisions. Rather than rely on one grand plan, they succeed through *an ecology of micro-adjustments*, where localised errors strengthen global outcomes.

This adaptive loop feeds into emotional anti-fragility. Most people absorb shocks as trauma—perceived violations of how the world *should* work. But anti-fragile people integrate them as information. They don't catastrophise volatility; they contextualise it. They know that adversity, properly metabolised, *compounds into wisdom*. Emotional anti-fragility is not numbness—it's the ability to engage discomfort without being dismantled by it.

Taleb often frames anti-fragility as an inversion. Instead of asking what makes us safe, ask what makes us stronger under stress. Instead of eliminating variability, ask how to make it pay us. This inversion flips the traditional logic of risk management. Rather than reducing exposure, it asks how to structure exposure so that *when stress inevitably arrives, you're not merely unharmed—you're better off than before.*

This concept has special resonance in an age of hyper-complexity. Systems are faster, more interconnected, and less predictable than ever before. Linear thinking is not just outdated—it's dangerous. Anti-fragile systems, by contrast, *expect the unexpected*, not in specific detail, but in structural logic. They are not brittle because they are not overconfident. They are not paralysed because they are not reactive. Their edge is structural, not situational.

For investors, the implication is clear: stop seeking safety through overcontrol. Start seeking *advantage through design*. Portfolio diversity, cash buffers, uncorrelated bets—these are not just defensive—they are strategic weapons in a stochastic world. For entrepreneurs, the lesson is to build businesses that can *gain from shocks*—where complexity is not a threat, but a substrate for innovation. And for individuals, the takeaway is equally clear: build habits, relationships, and systems that don't just survive the storm but *absorb its force and transform it into forward motion.*

Anti-fragility is not a slogan. It is a philosophy, a methodology, and a discipline. It invites us to replace the illusion of control with the *architecture of robustness plus upside*. It is about placing ourselves in a position where stress sharpens rather than shatters, where uncertainty becomes the input to growth, and where volatility is no longer feared—but *functionalised*. This is not about being unbreakable. It is about becoming better *because* we are breakable—so long as the break is bounded and the feedback loop intact. This is the advantage of the anti-fragile: not that they avoid stress, but that *they are improved by it.*

Training for Controlled Exposure

Most people approach risk like a hazard to be avoided rather than a muscle to be trained. This framing is not only unhelpful—it's strategically limiting. Emotional tolerance for volatility is not a fixed trait. Like physical resilience, it can be expanded through controlled exposure. The key is to stretch your psychological capacity deliberately, incrementally, and with full awareness—building your ability to remain composed, rational, and grounded while engaging with real uncertainty. Emotional endurance, particularly in the financial and strategic domains, is not about eliminating discomfort. It's about increasing the threshold at which discomfort distorts judgment.

Controlled exposure is a process of small, repeated rehearsals with risk that gradually inoculate the individual against emotional overreaction. In behavioural psychology, this is akin to desensitisation: by intentionally facing a stimulus in measured doses, the subject reduces their anxiety response. In financial behaviour, the same logic holds. A novice investor terrified of market corrections becomes less reactive after living through several—assuming those experiences were framed correctly. The objective isn't mere tolerance. It's *familiarisation with stress under non-destructive conditions*, so the nervous system no longer interprets normal volatility as existential threat.

This training must begin with self-awareness. Before introducing any exposure, the individual must identify their current thresholds: where does discomfort begin to compromise logic? Is it during temporary losses? Social comparison? Regret over missed opportunities? The training process depends on tailoring exposure to the emotional contours of the individual's specific vulnerabilities. A person prone to panic-selling may benefit from exercises in sitting through paper losses without intervention. Someone paralysed by the fear of public embarrassment may grow through calculated reputational risk—such as publishing a contrarian view or presenting unfinished ideas. *Emotional resilience grows in the presence of precision-targeted stress—not in its absence.*

One practical application is in micro-investing with volatility baked in. Allocating a small, non-essential sum into high-volatility assets—crypto, small-cap stocks, or leveraged ETFs—can provide a laboratory for learning. The point is not to outperform; it's to observe one's reactions. If a £1,000 investment drops 30% in a week, how does the body react? What internal narrative emerges? Can you watch the drop without impulsive action? The aim is to turn what would normally be a trigger into *data*, and to convert reaction into reflection. Over time, the brain learns to reclassify volatility from threat to information.

Another layer involves deliberate exposure to decision-making under conditions of incomplete information. Most people default to waiting for certainty—a delay that costs them agility and compounding. Instead, small bets with ambiguous outcomes—such as choosing between two career paths, projects, or investments with equal plausibility—can be a form of psychological strength training. Done repeatedly, the individual becomes more at ease making choices without perfect knowledge. This is critical. In reality, the most consequential decisions—where to live, whom to marry, whether to exit a role—are always made under conditions of risk. *Waiting for clarity is often a euphemism for paralysis.*

Controlled exposure can also take the form of cognitive discomfort—engaging consistently with ideas that challenge your worldview. Emotionally fragile thinkers avoid contradictory data. Emotionally robust individuals seek it out. Subscribe to publications with views you disagree with. Study investment theses that oppose your own. Not to concede, but to *fortify clarity through exposure to uncertainty*. When this practice becomes habitual, intellectual flexibility improves alongside emotional resilience.

Another underutilised tool is *public commitment to uncertain outcomes.* When an individual states a clear intention—writing a forecast, taking a public stance, or committing capital—they inject reputational risk into the system. This exposure intensifies emotional stakes. But it also sharpens thinking, tightens accountability, and forces internal calibration. Done at appropriate scale, this is not recklessness—it is *discipline under spotlight.* The discomfort teaches one to remain composed and analytic when performance anxiety would otherwise hijack cognition.

Controlled exposure also applies outside financial domains. If the goal is to increase tolerance for entrepreneurial risk, start a small side venture with defined downside. If the goal is to expand emotional courage in conversation, raise a difficult topic in a low-stakes setting. The principle remains constant: *strategic, bounded discomfort leads to growth.* What matters is that the exposure be intentional, repeated, and framed as training—not as proof of capability.

To optimise learning from exposure, reflection is essential. The act of facing volatility is not sufficient. It must be *processed.* After each deliberate exposure, whether emotional, financial, or reputational, write down what happened: what was the reaction, what narratives arose, what physical sensations, what rationalisations? Over time, this data creates a personalised map of triggers, allowing for tailored future exposures. *Self-knowledge accelerates emotional expansion.*

Of course, controlled exposure is not the same as tolerating abuse, gambling recklessly, or pushing through burnout. It is not a macho invitation to endure unnecessary pain. It is about *intelligent dosage*—calibrating the intensity of risk to stimulate adaptation without causing breakdown. Like strength training, the goal is to be challenged but not injured. Just as muscles grow from time under tension, emotional capital grows from *decisions made under mild to moderate stress—decisions that reinforce composure, not collapse.*

One of the most underestimated domains of training is time horizon discipline. Few stressors erode judgement faster than impatience. Individuals who practice holding to long-term strategies under short-term pressure develop an edge that is almost unfair. This can be trained in multiple ways: by manually lengthening the interval between checking your portfolio; by writing down your strategy and reading it before any decision; or by simulating historical scenarios (e.g., what would have happened had you sold during past corrections?). These exercises *recalibrate the internal clock*, which in most people is unfit for financial timeframes.

Ultimately, controlled exposure builds what ancient philosophers and modern behavioural scientists both recognise as indispensable: *non-reactivity*. The person who can act without being hijacked by transient emotion will outperform those who cannot, regardless of intelligence or resources. Controlled exposure is the crucible in which non-reactivity is forged. It is not glamorous. It is not tweetable. But it is durable. And in the domains that reward long-term compounding, durability beats intensity.

This approach is also scalable. At first, the exposures are small, even trivial. But each time the person chooses rational action over emotional impulse, a feedback loop is initiated. Confidence grows—not as bravado, but as *earned trust in one's own internal regulation.* Risk no longer feels like chaos. It feels like terrain. The peaks and troughs remain, but the walker is surefooted.

As controlled exposure continues, the threshold for emotional disruption rises. What once felt like a crisis becomes manageable. What was once unthinkable becomes routine. The goal is not fearlessness—that would be dangerous. The goal is fluency with fear. *To know it, name it, stay with it, and decide anyway.*

If risk is the price of all meaningful upside, then training for risk tolerance is not optional. It is the substrate of strategic advantage. And like any form of training, it rewards those who treat it as a craft. The emotionally untrained seek to eliminate risk. The trained seek to understand it, engage it, and benefit from it—not all at once, but *incrementally, deliberately, and with patience as their long-term leverage.*

Chapter 7
The Emotional Discipline of Investing

Most investment strategies don't implode because the arithmetic was flawed. They implode because the human carrying them out couldn't resist interfering. Markets are merciless with the impulsive, far more so than with the merely uninformed. At its most durable level, investing is less a test of brilliance than of composure. The rarest advantage is not privileged access to data, but emotional steadiness when the pressure mounts. And that, curiously, is the one skill that even the most educated investors often lack.

The rational framework for compounding wealth has been laid out time and again: buy quality assets, hold them over long horizons, reinvest intelligently. Nothing mysterious there. The real difficulty is execution—not once, but continuously—through stretches of monotony, the siren calls of temptation, the noise of pundits, the pangs of envy, the spikes of fear. Retail investors usually fail not for want of opportunity or intellect, but because they cannot manage their own behavioural volatility. This chapter isn't about new products or exotic instruments. It is about the psychological stance that allows returns to endure across time.

Let us begin with one of the most seductive myths in all of investing: timing the market. The fantasy of buying at the bottom and selling at the top flatters the mind and soothes the ego. But in practice, history reveals it to be ruinous. Research from Dalbar, tracking average investor returns against benchmarks, makes the point starkly: miss the ten best trading days in a decade, and your returns are cut in half. These "best days" almost always occur amid or immediately after violent volatility. Those who flinch are cut off from the compounding that does the heavy lifting.

But the real question isn't *that* people attempt timing—it's *why*. Emotional distortion, above all overconfidence, fear of missing out, and loss aversion, drives activity where patience would have sufficed. Consider the Dunning–Kruger effect: those with the least expertise often have the greatest confidence in their judgement. A streak of short-term wins fuels conviction, which soon hardens into reckless bets, frantic trades, or even leverage. Ironically, the more emotionally attached one becomes to a prediction, the less capacity there is to adapt when conditions change. Overconfidence doesn't just expose risk—it blinds.

Disciplined investors protect themselves by stripping discretion out of the process. One of the most effective tools is dollar-cost averaging: investing a fixed amount at set intervals, regardless of what the market is doing. Volatility becomes an ally, since one accumulates more when prices fall and less when they rise. More importantly, it bypasses the exhausting theatre of regret. "Should I have waited? Did I miss the bottom? Am I buying at the top?" These questions evaporate. The system has answered them in advance. Automation, in this sense, doubles as armour.

Yet emotional discipline isn't all about structured doing. It is equally about strategic not-doing—learning when inaction is the highest form of action. This is profoundly countercultural. In an age that glorifies hustle, restraint is misread as idleness. The record tells another story. Warren Buffett's typical holding period is measured not in weeks or months, but decades. Jack Bogle, Vanguard's founder, was famously against tactical manoeuvring. And Charlie Munger distilled it to a line: "The big money is not in the buying or the selling, but in the waiting." That was no philosophical garnish; it was strategy grounded in empirical reality.

Still, doing nothing is painfully difficult. It requires conviction that is internal, not borrowed from headlines or peer validation. It means withstanding noise, chatter, and creeping doubt. This is precisely where most falter—not in the presence of bad data, but in the presence of their own unease. Hence the insistence of this chapter: strategies are hollow without psychological conditioning. One must know, in advance, where one's emotional thresholds lie. Discovering them for the first time in the midst of crisis is too late.

The costs of emotional mismanagement are invisible, which makes them all the more destructive. Brokerage statements won't show the erosion from panic sales, excessive trading, or chasing a friend's "can't-miss" tip. Yet the toll accumulates. The so-called behavioural gap—the difference between market returns and actual investor returns—often dwarfs the spread between active and passive strategies. The flaw is not systemic; it is behavioural. And until that is recognised, nothing changes.

What separates the emotionally disciplined investor is not only temperament, but the systems they inhabit. Their environment is designed to blunt the sabotage of emotion: automated contributions, pre-set rules, a clear long-term orientation. Feelings are not eliminated—that is impossible—but their power to derail is dramatically curtailed. For such investors, discomfort is not a signal to pivot, but a signpost that they are still on the long road, while the crowd chases shortcuts.

The long road is tedious, which is precisely why it breaks so many. Restlessness, not panic, is the undoing of most. They fiddle, adjust, rotate, speculate—not because their strategy required it, but because stillness became unbearable. The irony is cruel: in seeking to optimise, they corrode the compounding they so desperately desire. True discipline is recognising when an urge to act is nothing more than that—an urge. Not a command.

This chapter traces the anatomy of emotional discipline. We begin by dismantling the fallacy of timing, then expose the hidden costs of overconfidence. We examine how automation—dollar-cost averaging chief among it—serves as a behavioural shield. And we conclude with a defence of patience: the highest-yield behaviour in investing, wrongly dismissed as passivity.

If there is one shift the reader should carry away, it is not tactical but temperamental. Move from seeking cleverness to building constancy. Because in the end, investing rewards not speed, nor bravado, nor intellectual gymnastics. It rewards the simple ability to keep doing the right thing, long enough, without interruption. Emotional discipline makes that possible. That, and nothing less, is its ultimate edge.

Time vs Timing

At the centre of nearly every failed investment plan is the same fatal assumption: that it is possible—and even necessary—to *know when.* When to buy, when to sell, when to switch strategies, when to go to cash. The seduction of timing the market is not merely financial—it is emotional. It flatters the ego, offers the illusion of control, and disguises itself as strategic thinking. Yet the historical data is unambiguous: *those who try to time the market are consistently outperformed by those who simply spend time in it.*

The appeal of market timing stems from a deep human discomfort with uncertainty. Investors crave narrative clarity—bull or bear, up or down, safe or dangerous—and in the absence of certainty, they substitute conviction. Analysts pontificate with precision, influencers broadcast confidence, and even seasoned professionals often feel compelled to act decisively, lest they appear unprepared. The market, meanwhile, continues to operate on a different plane—one defined not by predictions, but by probabilities. The greatest investors are not the best forecasters; they are the most emotionally stable participants.

Consider the empirical reality: between 1994 and 2023, the S&P 500 produced an annualised return of roughly 9.9%. Yet, if an investor missed just the ten best trading days during that 30-year span, their return dropped to 6.1%. Miss the best 20 days, and the return collapses to 3.9%. The pattern continues downward. These 'best days' are not randomly scattered; they tend to occur *during periods of peak uncertainty*. Investors who fled to safety in fear missed the very moments that generated long-term outperformance. *Timing is not merely difficult—it is structurally self-defeating.*

But the problem with market timing isn't just that it's rarely successful. It's that it *reorients the investor's psychology around precision rather than consistency*. Instead of asking, "How do I stay the course for decades?", the market timer begins asking, "Am I in or out this week?" This narrows the temporal lens, increases stress, and leads to performance-chasing. Every minor market fluctuation becomes a referendum on one's intelligence. The emotional tax is immense, and over time, corrosive.

By contrast, those who centre their strategy on *time in the market* benefit from the power of compounding—a force that, unlike human judgement, is consistent and predictable. The investor who begins early, contributes steadily, and avoids major interruptions will nearly always outperform the late-starting genius who attempts to be clever. This is not hypothetical. It's backed by real-world investor behaviour. Vanguard's internal data on investor accounts consistently show that those who trade less earn more. The reasons are clear: lower fees, fewer emotional mistakes, and uninterrupted compounding.

The discipline of long-term participation demands a philosophical shift: from being a tactician to being a builder. The tactician obsesses over micro-optimisations—getting in at the right point, anticipating downturns, reading economic tea leaves. The builder thinks in terms of decades, not days. They ask: What will this look like in 20 years? What am I building that will endure? This mental posture is not passive—it is strategic stillness. It is the understanding that *motion is not progress*, and that sometimes the most effective action is restraint.

Of course, disciplined participation is not about blind optimism. Markets do fall. Crashes happen. The global financial system is not immune to shocks. But the historical trajectory of human productivity and economic development has, for centuries, pointed upward. To be a long-term investor is not to deny risk—it is to accept it in context. It is to understand that *temporary volatility is the price of long-term growth*, and that trying to sidestep this price often results in forfeiting the reward.

This is where behavioural finance plays a critical role. The studies of Daniel Kahneman, Richard Thaler, and others have demonstrated that humans are poor at probabilistic thinking. We overweight recent experiences, anchor to emotionally salient data, and suffer from hindsight bias. We remember market crashes vividly, but we underappreciate the long recoveries that followed. We forget that the 2008 crash was followed by one of the longest bull markets in history. We panic in downturns because we fail to zoom out.

The myth of market timing also appeals because of a cultural bias toward action. We reward decisiveness. The investor who says "I moved to cash before the crash" is admired—even if they never re-entered the market and missed the rebound. The buy-and-hold investor, meanwhile, is perceived as boring, unreactive, or lazy. But in investing, *inactivity is often the highest form of wisdom*. The ability to *not act on emotion*—to simply let a sound strategy run its course—is a rarer and more valuable skill than any predictive ability.

Indeed, many of the world's most successful investors have internalised this insight. Warren Buffett, in countless shareholder letters, emphasises the importance of doing nothing most of the time. Charlie Munger often reminded audiences that the money is not made in the buying or the selling, but in the waiting. Jack Bogle founded Vanguard on the principle that attempting to outguess the market was futile and counterproductive. Their wealth was not built on timely brilliance. It was built on behavioural discipline.

Critically, the false dichotomy between time and timing must be dismantled. It is not that timing never works—it is that *it works far less often than people believe*, and usually by luck rather than skill. There are occasional success stories of perfect trades, but they are statistical outliers, not reproducible systems. And they create a dangerous illusion that distracts from the far more reliable engine of wealth creation: sustained exposure to quality assets, through all market conditions.

The argument, then, is not merely mathematical. It is *existential*. To commit to time over timing is to commit to a worldview—one that acknowledges randomness, accepts imperfection, and builds resilience. It means choosing peace over precision, probability over prediction, systems over stunts. It is the investor's equivalent of choosing health over short-term hacks, education over test-cramming, and craftsmanship over spectacle. It may not excite the media. But it builds quietly, relentlessly, and irreversibly.

Ultimately, successful investing is not about outsmarting the market. It is about outlasting it. That does not require a forecast. It requires a *framework*. A way of thinking that is robust under pressure, adaptive through change, and simple enough to execute without friction. Disciplined participation is not the absence of risk—it is the refusal to distort your plan in response to fear, greed, or noise. It is not market timing. It is *temporal maturity*.

If you are willing to give up the illusion of precision, the market has a reward system that is both brutal and fair. Brutal to the erratic. Fair to the patient. Over time, the difference between those who chase timing and those who compound quietly becomes exponential. One depends on being right once. The other only requires being *consistent*. That is the edge that lasts.

The Emotional Cost of Overconfidence

The greatest threat to investment performance is not market volatility, inflation, or even geopolitical risk. It is *ourselves*. Among the most destructive and underestimated forces in investing is overconfidence—an emotional and cognitive bias so pervasive that it quietly undermines even the most well-educated and analytically capable individuals. It is not merely an error in judgement; it is a distortion of self-perception, magnified by success and weaponised by access to information.

Overconfidence thrives in the illusion of control. It begins subtly: a few correct predictions, a streak of profitable trades, or a conviction that one has 'read' the market correctly. From this foundation grows the belief that skill, not chance, is the dominant variable. This belief is reinforced by selective memory—wins are internalised, losses are rationalised—and soon, a dangerous loop is created: the more confident we become, the more active we become; the more active we become, the more prone we are to costly mistakes.

The data is unequivocal. A landmark study by Brad Barber and Terrance Odean, analysing tens of thousands of retail brokerage accounts, found that the most active traders underperformed the market by significant margins—often by several percentage points annually. The less they traded, the better they did. Yet despite this, those who traded the most were the most confident in their abilities. *Confidence and competence, the study showed, were often inversely correlated.* The act of trading, rather than improving results, was frequently a manifestation of psychological discomfort: a compulsion to 'do something' in order to feel in control.

This need for action is partly rooted in evolutionary psychology. Human beings are wired to respond to uncertainty with decisive movement. In ancestral environments, passivity in the face of threat was often fatal. Today, that same impulse leads investors to overreact to short-term market noise, reallocate based on headlines, or chase momentum. Overconfidence fuels these responses by muting doubt—trading not as a calculated risk, but as a reflexive assertion of perceived insight.

Cognitive biases further reinforce the overconfidence trap. Confirmation bias drives investors to seek information that validates their existing beliefs, ignoring disconfirming evidence. Hindsight bias convinces them that past events were more predictable than they actually were, inflating their sense of foresight. Illusion of knowledge bias—the belief that more information necessarily leads to better decisions—pushes them to consume and act upon data without questioning its relevance or context. These biases do not operate in isolation; they compound and feed off each other, distorting both perception and behaviour.

The financial media plays a catalytic role in this dynamic. Constant streams of analysis, opinion, and prognostication create an environment of perceived urgency. Investors are conditioned to believe that every fluctuation demands a reaction. Meanwhile, those who remain inactive—who resist this psychological bait—are seen as disengaged or unresponsive. In reality, *strategic inaction is often the highest form of discipline*, especially when driven by clear, long-term frameworks rather than fear or inertia.

Consider the example of institutional investors. While they are equipped with resources, research teams, and algorithmic tools far beyond the reach of the average individual, they too are not immune to overconfidence. Studies consistently show that active fund managers, on average, underperform their benchmarks net of fees. A significant contributor is overestimation of their own edge. Even among the most sophisticated players, humility—not confidence—

is often the variable that separates enduring success from transient luck.

The emotional cost of overconfidence also manifests in volatility intolerance. When investors place trades rooted in conviction rather than probabilistic reasoning, they tie their self-worth to outcomes they cannot control. A bad trade becomes not just a financial loss but an existential blow. This amplifies stress, shortens time horizons, and erodes rational thinking. It becomes harder to hold onto long-term positions through drawdowns, harder to distinguish signal from noise, and harder to admit error. The psychological burden compounds the financial one.

This is why emotionally resilient investors are often the least reactive. They understand that the most dangerous trait in investing is not ignorance but *certainty*. They do not pretend to know what the market will do next quarter or next year. Instead, they focus on building systems that are robust to error, tolerant of randomness, and anchored in humility. Their confidence is not in prediction, but in process.

It is tempting to believe that education and intelligence inoculate one from overconfidence. But research suggests otherwise. Highly educated investors often suffer more from the illusion of control, precisely because they have been rewarded in other domains for analytical rigour and assertiveness. Markets, however, do not obey intellectual rules. They are probabilistic, not deterministic. They punish hubris with merciless efficiency. *The market does not care how smart you are; it cares how disciplined you are.*

The antidote to overconfidence is not passivity, but *awareness*. First, awareness of how little we can truly predict. The world is too complex, too dynamic, and too sensitive to non-linear events for any one person to forecast consistently. Second, awareness of our behavioural tendencies—the patterns of thought that seduce us into believing we have control where we do not. And third, awareness of process over outcome. A sound process can yield a poor result, just as a flawed process can occasionally produce success. The goal is not to eliminate error, but to build systems that perform *despite* error.

One powerful practice for combating overconfidence is reflective journaling. By documenting decisions before outcomes are known—recording the reasoning, assumptions, and emotions involved—investors can later assess whether their thinking was sound or simply lucky. This retrospective analysis builds metacognitive awareness: the ability to think about how we think. Over time, it tempers reactive impulses and instils a deeper respect for uncertainty.

Another effective approach is pre-mortem analysis. Instead of asking "Why will this investment succeed?", the investor asks "Assume this fails—why might that happen?" This forces the mind out of the default confirmation pattern and encourages rigorous scenario planning. It introduces doubt not as weakness, but as a strategic asset.

Ultimately, the emotional cost of overconfidence is not just poor returns—it is psychological fragility. It leaves the investor vulnerable to every market swing, every unexpected outcome, every missed opportunity. It corrodes the ability to endure, to learn, and to improve. The most durable investors are not those who believe most strongly in their own predictions, but those who remain steady when their predictions fail.

The disciplined investor cultivates what psychologist Carol Dweck termed a "growth mindset": a willingness to learn from failure, to adapt, to evolve. They understand that markets are not puzzles to be solved, but ecosystems to be navigated. And navigation requires not bravado, but balance. Not certainty, but self-regulation.

Confidence is not inherently dangerous. But when unmoored from feedback, humility, and probabilistic thinking, it becomes a liability. To invest well over the long term is not to eliminate confidence, but to *channel it through systems* that do not depend on perfect foresight. It is to recognise that our greatest edge is not our intellect, but our ability to remain clear-headed in the face of complexity.

Overconfidence makes us feel strong. But emotional discipline is what keeps us strong. The difference is not semantic. It is the boundary between noise and wisdom, action and insight, fragility and resilience. And over time, it is the difference between merely participating in markets and mastering the game they represent.

Dollar-Cost Averaging as Emotional Armor

One of the most quietly effective investing strategies is also among the least exciting. It doesn't involve exotic asset classes, advanced modelling, or the adrenaline rush of timing a market bottom. It demands no brilliance, minimal judgement, and little reactivity. And yet, for long-term wealth creation, few tools are as reliable—or as psychologically protective—as dollar-cost averaging (DCA). This simple, systematic method of investing fixed amounts at regular intervals functions not just as a financial mechanism, but as an *emotional firewall* against the cognitive traps that sabotage most investors.

At its core, DCA is a behavioural discipline disguised as a financial strategy. It removes timing from the equation by automating contributions, ensuring that money is invested regardless of market conditions. When prices are high, the same amount buys fewer units; when prices fall, it buys more. Over time, this levels out the average cost of acquisition and smooths out the psychological burden of decision-making. But more critically, DCA builds *emotional resilience.* It insulates the investor from the noise of short-term volatility and the paralysing fear of making the 'wrong' move.

The brilliance of DCA lies not in its ability to maximise short-term returns—there are more aggressive strategies that may outperform in hindsight—but in its capacity to *optimise investor behaviour.* The average investor does not underperform because of poor tools or insufficient knowledge, but because of poor decisions driven by emotion: chasing momentum, bailing out during crashes, overreacting to headlines. DCA counteracts this by anchoring action to habit, not impulse.

To understand its impact, consider investor behaviour during major market events. The COVID-19 crash of March 2020 was swift and brutal. Global equities fell over 30% in a matter of weeks. Headlines screamed collapse. Many panicked investors pulled out, crystallising losses that would have been avoided had they stayed the course. Those employing DCA, however, were mechanically buying into that decline—acquiring more units at discounted prices, even as others fled. When markets rebounded sharply in the months that followed, these automated purchases became the highest-performing entries in their portfolios. The emotional discipline required to buy during a panic is substantial; DCA sidesteps this requirement entirely by making the decision *before* the emotion arises.

This is where DCA transcends its mathematical simplicity and becomes a form of emotional architecture. It removes the burden of choice during periods of uncertainty. It says: *you do not need to be brave or brilliant or clairvoyant—you just need to show up consistently.* That consistency is the investor's true edge, because the market is not a test of intelligence—it is a test of temperament. In fact, most investors are not competing against each other; they are competing against their own worst impulses. DCA is how one plays the game with fewer opportunities for self-sabotage.

Critics of DCA often point out that lump-sum investing (LSI), when capital is available, has historically outperformed DCA more often than not. This is true—statistically, markets trend upward over time, so deploying funds early tends to result in greater compounding. But this critique misses the point. The superiority of LSI is theoretical; its practicality is deeply flawed. *Most investors do not have large lump sums to deploy, nor the emotional stamina to withstand watching that lump sum drop 15% the following week.* More importantly, the data assumes rational actors with infinite conviction—an assumption that collapses under real-world stress. For the average investor, LSI may produce higher returns *if they stay invested.* DCA increases the odds that they actually will.

Behavioural finance, as pioneered by scholars like Daniel Kahneman and Richard Thaler, repeatedly demonstrates that investors systematically act against their own interests under stress. Loss aversion—the tendency to feel the pain of losses more acutely than the pleasure of equivalent gains—causes people to exit positions prematurely. Recency bias convinces them that current trends will continue indefinitely. Overconfidence leads to unnecessary meddling. DCA, by embedding discipline into process, neutralises these biases at the operational level. The investor no longer needs to rely on willpower; they've installed a system that works without emotional consent.

From a philosophical standpoint, DCA aligns with a posture of humility. It acknowledges that *we do not know when the best time to invest is*. Rather than attempting to outsmart the market, it accepts the futility of prediction and opts instead for persistent participation. This is not passive investing; it is *principled investing*. It's a quiet rejection of the illusion of control, a statement that time—not timing—is the lever of wealth creation. In this way, DCA fosters not only better returns, but better character: patience, steadiness, and a bias toward action through systems rather than opinions.

The automation aspect of DCA is particularly crucial. By removing friction from the process—whether through payroll deductions, direct debit instructions, or recurring transfers—the strategy moves from idea to infrastructure. There is no deliberation each month, no evaluation of whether now is a good time. It *just happens*. This is one of the most underappreciated benefits: it reduces the frequency of decision-making, and therefore the number of opportunities to make a poor decision. As investor Morgan Housel notes, "The ability to do nothing is often underrated." DCA encodes that principle into the system.

Some critics argue that DCA can lead to underperformance if markets move sharply upward without correction. That may be true in specific bull runs. But again, *the goal is not to optimise for maximum gains in every scenario; it's to optimise for sustainable gains across volatile conditions*. It's to build a process that works when the environment is messy, uncertain, or emotionally charged—which is *most of the time*. If a strategy allows the investor to remain invested through crashes, recessions, and mania phases, it has already succeeded in preserving the most critical variable in long-term success: uninterrupted exposure.

Real-world application of DCA extends beyond equities. It can be applied to property funds, retirement schemes, ETFs, and even Bitcoin or other speculative assets—provided the individual understands the long-term nature and volatility profile of the asset.

Crucially, DCA is *not* a substitute for due diligence. It should not be used to drip-feed capital into unsound investments. But within a diversified, low-cost, long-term portfolio, DCA can act as the ballast that steadies the investor during storms.

The behavioural benefit of DCA also extends to post-investment monitoring. Because the investor is focused on process rather than timing, there is less temptation to obsess over daily price movements or short-term underperformance. The lens shifts from prediction to participation. This reduces anxiety, fosters long-term thinking, and creates the space for compounding to work its silent magic.

It's worth noting that DCA is also scalable. It works for the beginner investing £100 a month and for the seasoned professional allocating hundreds of thousands in stages. It is a framework, not a fixed prescription. Its value lies in its psychological design: it forces consistency, reduces regret, and builds a sense of identity around discipline. Over time, this builds emotional capital as surely as it builds financial capital.

Perhaps the most powerful aspect of DCA is what it symbolises. It is a quiet declaration of faith—not in any particular asset or market cycle, but in *process over prediction, in action over anxiety, and in long-term alignment over short-term optimisation.* For the investor who understands this, DCA is not just a strategy. It is a philosophy of participation, resilience, and self-regulation.

Wealth, at its most enduring level, is rarely built through bursts of brilliance. It is accumulated through rhythm, restraint, and rigour. Dollar-cost averaging, far from being a passive fallback, represents a high form of discipline. It is the armour that protects the investor not just from markets, but from themselves. And in a world where noise is constant and reaction is currency, that armour may be the most valuable asset of all.

Knowing When to Do Nothing

In a culture obsessed with hustle, movement, and decisive action, the discipline of doing nothing is often dismissed as passivity. Yet in the context of long-term investing, *knowing when to remain still* may be one of the most underappreciated—and misunderstood—skills of all. The instinct to intervene, to optimise, to "do something" can be powerfully seductive. But acting simply to relieve discomfort or to satisfy the illusion of control is often the very thing that undermines performance. Some of the most successful investors in history have not distinguished themselves by relentless activity, but by the *strategic restraint* to sit still when others scrambled.

The irony of modern investing is that technological progress has made it easier than ever to act impulsively—24/7 trading platforms, algorithmic alerts, real-time data streams. The barrier to executing trades has collapsed. But while access has been democratised, *discipline has not.* The ease with which one can now buy, sell, rebalance or reshuffle has become an emotional liability, tempting investors to act more frequently than their knowledge justifies. Every news cycle seems to demand a response. Yet over time, those who resist the urge to respond often outperform those who can't help but tinker.

Warren Buffett, often cited and rarely emulated, has described the stock market as a mechanism designed to transfer wealth from the active to the patient. His own investment record is less a product of genius-level timing than of *extraordinary inertia.* For decades, Berkshire Hathaway's success has rested not on hundreds of bold trades, but on a small number of enduring bets—many of which have been held through multiple cycles of economic panic, sector rotation and technological disruption. Buffett's success stems less from what he knows and more from what he's willing to ignore. *The willingness to do nothing is not laziness; it is mastery over ego, fear and noise.*

But this principle extends far beyond iconic investors. A Vanguard study of retirement account holders found that those who checked their portfolios the least frequently also tended to achieve higher average returns. Why? Because they were less likely to react emotionally to short-term volatility. They didn't sell after a dip or rotate into hot sectors. They allowed time and compounding to work. What looks like neglect is often restraint in disguise. And what looks like attention is often hyperactivity masquerading as prudence.

This is not an argument for disengagement or ignorance. Doing nothing is not the same as *being uninformed.* It is not a call to ignore relevant data, nor to abdicate responsibility. It is a strategic stance—a conscious rejection of overreaction, a deliberate avoidance of reflexive action. The emotional challenge lies in distinguishing between *necessary action and compulsive reaction.* Knowing when to do nothing requires clarity of intent, not a lack of involvement.

Consider the 2008 financial crisis. Many retail investors, spooked by plunging markets and media-fuelled panic, sold into weakness—realising steep losses just before a generational rebound. Yet those who sat still—who kept contributing to their pension funds, who didn't reallocate based on fear—benefited massively from the recovery. A decade later, they were not only made whole, but meaningfully ahead. Doing nothing, in the moment, may have felt irresponsible or even naïve. In hindsight, it was precisely the right move.

The behavioural finance literature is unequivocal: the average investor's underperformance relative to the market is primarily due to mistimed moves, not poor asset selection. Dalbar's long-running quantitative analysis has repeatedly shown that investors underperform their own investments—meaning the very funds they buy do better than the investors who hold them. The gap is driven not by fees or strategy, but by *emotional churn.* Investors buy high, sell low, and switch strategies at the worst possible times. Doing nothing would have closed the gap.

From a psychological standpoint, inaction is hard because it *feels irresponsible.* It provides no illusion of agency. It is quiet in a world that rewards noise. But precisely because it is emotionally counterintuitive, it must often be chosen *deliberately.* This is what distinguishes strategic patience from passive neglect. One is indifference; the other is emotional mastery. *To do nothing when doing something would soothe your anxiety—that is a power move.*

This mindset is echoed by some of the best institutional investors. Howard Marks, co-founder of Oaktree Capital, has noted that most investment errors don't come from decisions made too late, but from decisions made too early. Premature reactions, especially to macro events, often prove costly. Markets are complex, adaptive systems. They do not reward clairvoyance as much as they punish *overreach.* The discipline to wait, to observe without acting, is often the investor's greatest edge.

Even within algorithmic and quantitative trading firms—environments stereotyped as hyperactive—the most effective strategies often revolve around *limiting trades.* High-frequency execution is not synonymous with high emotional frequency. The logic is clear: every decision is a potential point of failure. Reducing the total number of decisions reduces error exposure. In the realm of personal investing, where decisions are made by emotionally fallible humans, the imperative to minimise unnecessary action is even greater.

There's also a structural case for inaction. The tax efficiency of long-term holding is often substantial. Frequent trading realises gains, generating short-term capital tax liabilities. By contrast, sitting still defers tax, allowing compounding to occur on a larger base. The math is clear: *not acting can be a financial advantage*, not just a behavioural one.

Still, none of this makes inaction emotionally easy. When markets are rising sharply, sitting still feels like missed opportunity. When markets are falling, it feels like willful neglect. And in sideways markets, it feels like stagnation. But beneath that discomfort lies a fundamental truth: *activity and progress are not synonymous.* In investing, time is the engine of returns—not action. And the role of the investor is to *stay aligned with time*, not to outmanoeuvre it.

Charlie Munger, Buffett's long-time partner, once said that the big money is not in the buying or the selling, but in the waiting. This isn't a platitude—it's a framework. Great investors don't just know when to buy and sell; they know *when to wait.* They design systems, portfolios and mindsets that allow them to endure periods of stillness with confidence. Their portfolios are less a reflection of current news, and more a reflection of accumulated wisdom—of decisions *not* taken, of distractions resisted.

But perhaps the most important insight is this: doing nothing is a form of action. It is a choice. And like all important choices, it must be grounded in clarity, conviction and self-awareness. *Stillness is not the absence of strategy—it is the expression of strategic maturity.* It is the investor stepping back from the noise and saying: "I have already decided. I am already positioned. I do not need to act simply to feel in control."

In a financial world saturated with stimulation—push notifications, expert forecasts, flashing dashboards—the ability to do nothing is not weakness. It is power. It is the power to resist noise, to defer gratification, to remain faithful to process over prediction. And over time, it is this power that separates those who build enduring wealth from those who merely chase it.

To know when to do nothing is to know yourself: your triggers, your insecurities, your illusions of control. It is to master *the emotional architecture of patience*, and to embed that mastery not just in philosophy, but in action—or deliberate inaction. In the final analysis, it is not what we do in markets that defines our results. It is often what we *resist doing* when we are most tempted to act.

Chapter 8
The Patience Dividend in Career and Business

If compounding is finance's loudest force, then patience is its quieter sibling in the realm of career and enterprise. The glamour of overnight triumphs and breathless startup legends obscures a slower, less visible truth: genuine professional value accrues beneath the surface, grain by grain. Mastery, credibility, reputation, strategic footing—none of these arrive in a single lightning strike. They belong to those who resist distraction long enough to let time work. Patience in work is not passivity; it is discipline, applied under pressure, against the grain of urgency.

Yet today's professional culture glorifies immediacy. "Scale fast or die." "Fail fast, fail often." "You're one viral post away from a different life." The slogans are seductive, fed by a world that can broadcast and monetise in seconds. And still, the careers and companies that endure tell a subtler story: the ones who earn respect, the entrepreneurs who outlast cycles, the firms that survive disruption—they are builders of duration, not sprinters for attention. Speed dazzles. Duration earns trust. And trust, unlike metrics of exposure, compounds.

Think of mastery itself. Skill-building does not trace a neat curve. Early hours spent reading, rehearsing, presenting, coding, failing—look fruitless on the surface. Nothing "happens." But something subterranean does: instinctive fluency, judgement, contextual grasp. Years later, a decision made in seconds is underwritten by thousands of such invisible deposits. This is why patience in craft is leverage. Short-term thinkers hunt outcomes. The patient accumulate capabilities that silently tilt the field.

The difficulty is emotional. At the start of a career, patience feels like stagnation. No title yet, no platform, no evidence to wave around. Peers seem to vault ahead. In such moments, patience feels like paying a tax—hard to bear, harder to explain. But it is often in precisely these stretches, when recognition is thin and progress feels abstract, that long-term advantage is actually being laid down. Not legible on a CV, but unavoidable in the arc of years.

Optionality—the power to pivot or seize high-stakes opportunities—rarely comes from chasing novelty. It grows out of patiently layering value: integrity, skill, networks, perspective. The supposed "overnight" ascents of figures like Satya Nadella or Susan Wojcicki were decades in the making. Both served long apprenticeships within their organisations before stepping into leadership. Their rise was built not on exposure, but on trust patiently compounded. Institutions rarely gamble on the flashy self-promoter. They favour those who practised strategic restraint.

The entrepreneurial world confirms this. Unicorn headlines may fill the feed, but the companies that endure economic winters are built by founders who prefer resilience to drama. Patagonia became iconic not through explosive tactics but through decades of values-led steadiness. Shopify, before it was a household name, was understated, "boring" even, focused on infrastructure rather than buzz. Its founder, Tobias Lütke, once remarked: "The most successful people I know are all very, very patient." He wasn't issuing a platitude. He was outlining a model.

Patience in business means honouring feedback loops that take years, sometimes decades. It means declining tempting capital, resisting premature expansion, refusing to hollow out the foundation in pursuit of quarterly gains. Crucially, it leaves space for markets to reveal themselves rather than trying to strong-arm them into predictability. Those who can wait do not fear competition as the impatient do; they recognise that most firms self-destruct from speed-induced fragility.

Perhaps the most underappreciated strategic skill—across both career and business—is the art of saying no. Declining a glittering offer, ignoring a trend, walking away from misaligned partnerships. Not because such opportunities are worthless, but because they bind you to the wrong timeline. The patient professional optimises not for applause, but for alignment. The quick yes is often fuelled by fear; the deliberate no, by clarity.

This stands in sharp relief against the fever of professional FOMO. The cultural whisper insists that if you don't pivot now, you'll be stranded. If you don't build your brand this year, you'll vanish. But the truth is less frantic. Long-game players are rarely conspicuous in their early innings. They bet slowly, build steadily, and accept obscurity as the price of durable influence. They know that nothing compounds if constantly reset.

Patience, applied over years, also builds resilience. A career built on credibility survives a stumble. A business rooted in trust can weather a crisis. Patience doesn't immunise against risk, but it distributes fragility across time, making recovery possible. Impatience does the opposite: it magnifies vulnerability, concentrates risk, and collapses under stress.

Over time, patience also hardens into clarity. The patient professional is not tugged this way and that by every market shift. They move from conviction, not from compulsion. This internal compass becomes armour. They are less manipulable, more selective, harder to shake. The paradox is that such clarity attracts opportunity. When you no longer chase relevance, relevance has a way of seeking you.

Patience, then, is not stillness. It is momentum measured in decades rather than quarters. It is choosing depth over velocity. Its gains arrive quietly but hold fast once they do. In a culture hooked on perception, patience is asymmetry: while others flame out, the patient accumulate. While others pivot endlessly, they dig roots. While others chase novelty, they thicken substance.

This chapter turns to that very discipline: how to build a career or business that survives the volatility of ambition. It looks at how to structure decisions, cultivate environments, and design habits so that time becomes an ally, not a threat. And it challenges the assumption that progress must always be visible, dramatic, externally validated. Often, the surest progress is seen in what no longer seduces you.

The dividends of patience are real, though unevenly distributed. They accrue only to those who think in decades, not seasons; who prioritise endurance over spectacle; who measure success by depth rather than noise. This is not moralising—it is strategy. Because in the end, the compounding belongs to those who stay long enough to let it work.

The Slow Build of Mastery

Mastery does not announce itself with trumpets. It arrives quietly—often after years of unnoticed labour, deliberate iteration, and emotional restraint. It is not the consequence of passion alone or talent in isolation, but the patient alignment of attention, repetition, and long-term orientation. In an age obsessed with speed and visibility, this idea is almost radical: that the most potent forms of success—skill, reputation, and enterprise—are not hacked into existence but *compounded into form*, over time, by people who resist the lure of shortcuts.

What distinguishes those who develop true mastery is not superior intellect or greater access, but a deeper willingness to delay emotional rewards in favour of structural gains. Emotional patience, in this context, is not a soft virtue. It is a strategic edge. It allows one to remain with complexity long enough to decode it. It grants permission to fail in private before succeeding in public. It gives the practitioner time to absorb nuance, to refine intuition, and to build fluency in domains where superficial effort yields nothing. *Mastery is not simply expertise; it is earned comfort with difficulty sustained over time.*

The early stages of mastery are marked not by breakthroughs but by frustration. Skill development is lumpy and opaque. You study, practise, and iterate without visible improvement. It's precisely at this stage that emotional impatience derails most people. They change lanes, declare themselves untalented, or pivot prematurely. What they miss is that slow starts are not signs of futility—they are *predictable features of deep competence formation.* You cannot skip the latency period of skill compounding. Trying to do so leads to brittle fluency: knowledge that looks impressive but collapses under complexity.

Take the example of professional chess. Grandmasters do not emerge from raw talent alone. They spend thousands of hours internalising not just tactics, but *patterns that only emerge over long exposure.* They develop what's known as "chunking"—the ability to rapidly assess complex positions based on countless mental models built from prior games. This isn't taught directly. It emerges only when a player stays in the game long enough for time to *translate knowledge into judgment.* This same process plays out in business, law, programming, architecture—any domain with real depth.

Patience is not about waiting; it's about sustained, intelligent action under uncertainty. In craftsmanship, for instance, true artisans don't merely repeat motions. They refine each iteration, compare outcomes, and embed improvement into their muscle memory. This cumulative method, often imperceptible to outsiders, is what distinguishes a functional designer from a master craftsman. There are no dramatic leaps—only microscopic optimisations repeated until the result becomes elegant. *What looks like genius is often process, tolerated for longer than most are willing to endure.*

In business, too, this principle holds. The most respected firms—those with enduring influence—are rarely built on viral moments or first-mover advantages. They are constructed through operational patience, where systems are strengthened over time and growth is driven by reputation, not hype. Consider Berkshire Hathaway. Warren Buffett did not make his fortune by racing to every opportunity; he made it by *waiting, watching, and acting only when the odds were heavily in his favour.* That decision-making rigour was paired with a temperament that could *tolerate boredom in the name of compounding.* His wealth, famously, is a function not only of investment insight but of *duration.* Mastery in his case wasn't just intellectual—it was emotional.

This dynamic is mirrored in the reputational domain. In the early years of a professional life, recognition is sparse. There is often little external validation for doing the right thing consistently—delivering on time, saying no to shortcuts, focusing on substance. But over time, these decisions accumulate. A track record forms. People start to refer others to you. Not because you marketed yourself well, but because you *became trustworthy by being consistent when no one was watching.* Reputation, like capital, compounds slowly—but once established, it provides leverage that raw skill cannot match.

In contrast, those who seek rapid ascension often pay invisible costs. The pursuit of quick wins tends to generate overexposure before one's foundations are fully formed. Early acclaim can trap a person into performance rather than improvement. They become defensive, performative, fragile. True mastery requires *failure in privacy*, the kind that refines skill without threatening ego. The emotionally patient are willing to forgo immediate applause to ensure their competence is real, durable, and transferable.

There is also an ethical dimension to the slow build. Patience tends to produce not only more resilient professionals, but *more principled ones*. When you are not constantly chasing the next opportunity, you gain the space to make value-aligned decisions. You can choose projects that stretch your abilities, rather than inflate your image. You can engage in partnerships that compound, rather than merely transact. You can say no—not from fear or arrogance, but from clarity. Patience is not only a financial virtue; it is a moral one, allowing your work to reflect integrity rather than desperation.

The modern obsession with scale tends to obscure this. Platforms reward virality over substance. Social media flattens expertise, giving visibility to those who are loud rather than deep. The temptation is to mimic what gets attention, even if it undermines your growth. But long-term success rarely comes from chasing attention. It comes from *doing the deep work long enough that attention eventually arrives as a side effect, not a goal.* Those who master a craft quietly often find that the world catches up later. And when it does, they're ready—not because they changed to meet the moment, but because they *stayed long enough to become undeniable.*

The psychological architecture required to endure this path is not accidental. It must be developed. You need routines that reinforce consistency, relationships that reward long-term thinking, and mental models that make boredom tolerable rather than threatening. One of the most effective is the idea of *lagging indicators*. The best results in life—reputation, mastery, wealth, impact—lag far behind the actions that generate them. Understanding this helps you decouple emotional reward from output. You don't feel good because you're winning; you feel good because you're *aligned with a system that will win eventually.*

This orientation also reduces anxiety. When you know that progress is nonlinear, you are less shaken by flat months or quiet seasons. You no longer measure your work against short-term metrics. You begin to trust *trajectory over immediate reward.* This doesn't mean you become passive—it means your urgency is directed toward the process, not the outcome. You don't ask, "Did this make a difference today?" You ask, "Is this a high-leverage action, even if no one sees it yet?"

Ultimately, the slow build of mastery is not just a professional framework; it is a philosophical stance. It requires you to define success on your own terms, to reject the borrowed timelines of others, and to orient your effort around durability rather than drama. It is, in essence, a quiet rebellion against the tyranny of urgency. In a culture that prizes acceleration, you choose traction. In a system that rewards output, you prioritise depth. And in doing so, you trade visibility for power, applause for competence, and quick wins for lasting edge.

The dividends of this approach are rarely immediate. But they are real. They show up in the freedom to choose your work, in the credibility that precedes you, and in the quiet confidence that you've built something unshakeable—not because you rushed, but because you *stayed.*

The Career Optionality Curve

The smartest long-term strategy in any modern career is not linear advancement. It is optionality—the gradual construction of privileges, skills, and reputational leverage that gives you more and better choices over time. Unlike conventional career planning, which often resembles climbing a ladder, the most durable trajectories resemble branching trees. Each deliberate, patient decision compounds to widen the arc of what becomes possible, even if those gains remain invisible for years. *Optionality is not about doing more; it is about increasing the quality and range of what you are able to choose later—by doing the right things now, with emotional discipline and delayed gratification.*

At first glance, many professional decisions appear to be equivalent: two jobs, two promotions, two projects. But their long-term asymmetry becomes obvious when viewed through the lens of compounding choice. One decision builds depth and future leverage; the other might offer temporary excitement but no structural advantage. The emotionally impatient optimise for immediate validation—bigger title, faster growth, louder environment. But those who understand the *optionality curve* make a different wager: that slow, strategic compounding of skills, networks, and trust capital can produce an exponential expansion of freedom, earnings, and impact in the decades to come.

Optionality is cumulative, not additive. And its engine is patience. A generalist jumping laterally every eighteen months may appear dynamic, but often ends up with fragmented expertise and shallow trust. By contrast, the professional who commits deeply—who studies the system, understands its stakeholders, tolerates the early grind, and contributes meaningfully—eventually becomes a *node of influence.* At that stage, options begin to self-generate. You are not just given opportunities—you are trusted to define them. The trap for the ambitious is thinking that visible motion equals meaningful progress. But *optionality accrues to those willing to invest quietly when nothing seems to be happening.*

In the early career phase, this discipline is especially difficult. Everyone wants to "move fast," to gain exposure, to pivot. But too much movement kills momentum. What looks like curiosity may actually be indecision. What looks like breadth might mask the absence of compoundable depth. If your early years are spent chasing novelty, you rob yourself of the hidden compounding that happens when you master the boring parts of a domain. It's only after years of close exposure that you begin to see the real structural levers. And it's those who can act on *deep context*, not surface trends, who end up writing the playbook others follow.

This is not a plea for stagnation. It is a recalibration of tempo. There is a difference between being stuck and being stable. Between being loyal and being deliberate. You can change roles, even change fields—but it matters *why* and *when.* Do you move because something better is being pulled toward you by the quality of your work? Or because you can't tolerate being early in the curve, where progress is slow but real? The test is whether your moves accumulate into leverage, or simply restart the clock.

Optionality, then, is not found—it is built. It is created through decisions that seem modest at the time: becoming excellent at something obscure; taking a difficult boss because they stretch you; joining a slow-moving company where deep process experience is possible; refusing to monetise too early because you're still building real insight. These actions don't pay off in quarters—they pay off in decades. But when they do, the compounding is astonishing. *You become the person others must call, not just the one they can call.*

One of the most powerful forces in career optionality is reputation. And reputation is notoriously slow to form. Early in a career, you are often hired for potential. But later, you are called for trust. Your name becomes a proxy for quality, reliability, and discernment. That trust cannot be gamed. It cannot be faked. It is the reward for *years of consistent decisions made when no one was watching.* Patience here means resisting the urge to embellish, over-promise, or over-market. It means anchoring your self-worth to contribution, not status. It means understanding that *real careers are not built in sprints—they are architected like cathedrals, stone by stone, over a lifetime.*

The most respected operators in any industry tend to share a peculiar trait: they're not in a rush, but they're never idle. They're always building something that fits their long-term view of where the world is going—and their place in it. That alignment, cultivated over years, gives their work clarity and weight. Their names carry strategic value. They are less likely to be hired for a job and more likely to be invited into conversations where jobs are created. That is the heart of optionality: not choosing from existing paths, but having the influence and freedom to shape new ones.

This principle is particularly powerful in fields shaped by volatility—tech, media, entrepreneurship, finance. These domains are prone to fads and bubbles, and it is tempting to chase the next big thing. But the greatest returns almost always accrue to those who *stay long enough to become differentiated while others are distracted.* Consider how often short-term hype devours long-term judgment. The founder who jumps from startup to startup never accumulates operational depth.

The investor who chases momentum misses the deep understanding of fundamentals. But the professional who endures the slow, often invisible process of compound learning eventually becomes unreplaceable.

Take Satya Nadella at Microsoft. He spent over two decades inside the company before becoming CEO. That kind of tenure is increasingly rare, but it enabled him to understand Microsoft's technical DNA, political architecture, and cultural inertia in a way that external candidates never could. His long-view thinking allowed him to reposition the company not by blowing it up, but by aligning its assets with the future. Nadella is an example of what optionality looks like *when compounded through patient strategic positioning within a complex system.*

Or consider the late-career pivots of individuals like Angela Duckworth, who left a high-intensity teaching and consulting career to pursue psychology research in mid-life, eventually producing the influential work on grit. Her early career was not wasted—it was *foundational.* It gave her questions worth answering and perspective others lacked. When she re-entered academia, she had a durable, differentiated lens—one that gave her career optionality through intellectual leverage. This is the essence of long-term positioning: *use the early years to absorb, the middle years to refine, and the later years to lead.*

Career optionality also means knowing when *not* to optimise. The person who maximises every decision for short-term gain often trades away invisible long-term options. Saying no to certain opportunities—especially lucrative but misaligned ones—can preserve your capacity to take bigger bets later. The ability to say no is one of the most overlooked forms of career power, and it is only available to those who have built a solid foundation beneath them. You cannot say no from weakness. You must say no from surplus—of skill, of savings, of clarity.

To do this well, one must build what philosopher-novelist Robert Pirsig called *"value traps."* These are commitments that narrow your choices in the short term so that you can unlock greater meaning and influence later. They include things like pursuing depth over breadth, taking ownership when it's uncomfortable, or learning a craft before selling it. These constraints are not limitations—they are *design choices* that force coherence. Over time, they produce careers that are both economically resilient and psychologically fulfilling.

A final point: the compounding of career options is not just individual. It is relational. The best opportunities often come through *networks of trust*, not applications. And trust networks form slowly. They require reciprocity, generosity, and patience. The person who helps others early, without expectation, often finds themselves with doors open decades later. Not because they asked—but because they *invested in goodwill long before they needed it.* Relationships, like skills, compound. And their dividends are highest when nurtured patiently and without agenda.

So while the world shouts urgency, the optionality curve whispers a different truth: that the most powerful careers are built quietly, with emotional patience, structural thoughtfulness, and strategic restraint. Every job you accept, every project you commit to, every habit you form—it either narrows or expands your future possibilities. Choose with the long arc in mind. Not just what gets you there fastest, but what gives you *the most valuable set of next moves when the stakes are higher and the spotlight is brighter.*

Because eventually, it's not just about having a job. It's about being the person whose choices create the conditions where the best work of your life becomes not only possible—but inevitable.

Entrepreneurship as an Endurance Game

There is a fundamental tension at the heart of modern entrepreneurship: the difference between *starting up* and *staying in.* The contemporary business culture, shaped by venture capital mythology and social media storytelling, often idolises the founder who scales fast, exits early, and disrupts loudly. But beneath the glamour of unicorn valuations and glossy pitch decks lies a quieter, less celebrated reality—*enduring entrepreneurship.* The kind that compounds year after year, not by chasing the next round of funding, but by patiently refining operations, building customer trust, and mastering a market's nuances. If startup hype is a sprint, enduring entrepreneurship is a multi-decade ultramarathon. It rewards stamina over spectacle, restraint over reaction, and clarity over charisma.

Short-term hype is structurally seductive. It promises scale without friction, recognition without proof, and wealth without weathering discomfort. This is especially alluring to new entrepreneurs, who face enormous pressure to move quickly, optimise for growth metrics, and demonstrate traction in ever-shortening timeframes. But very often, what looks like acceleration is simply burn rate—money, energy, and credibility consumed in pursuit of an exit rather than a durable business. Startups flame out not because their ideas are bad, but because their timelines are unrealistic. *Speed, misapplied, is a liability.*

Endurance-based entrepreneurship, by contrast, accepts uncertainty as a permanent feature of the terrain. It is built on emotional patience and long feedback loops. It requires a tolerance for obscurity, an indifference to fads, and a commitment to solving real problems for real people—again and again, even when it's not exciting. The entrepreneurs who play this longer game understand that *trust takes time, and trust is the ultimate moat.* They don't just launch—they listen. They don't just pivot—they persist.

Consider the story of Patagonia, founded by Yvon Chouinard. For decades, the company grew at a deliberate pace, reinvesting profits, avoiding debt, and making deeply principled decisions that often ran counter to prevailing business trends. Chouinard famously referred to himself as a "reluctant businessman," but in practice, his long-term orientation created one of the most respected and resilient brands in the world. Patagonia's success did not come from rushing product cycles or maximising investor returns. It came from *deep coherence between mission, culture, and execution*—maintained consistently over time. Few startups could sustain that kind of clarity under the pressure of quarterly reporting and liquidity demands.

Or take the example of Basecamp, the Chicago-based software company founded by Jason Fried and David Heinemeier Hansson. In a tech landscape obsessed with hypergrowth, Basecamp chose to remain small, profitable, and focused. They raised a modest amount of outside capital once, declined to pursue aggressive scaling, and built a loyal customer base by delivering stable, thoughtfully designed products. Their approach has often been dismissed as "lifestyle business" strategy. But that criticism misunderstands the deeper principle: *a business should serve the lives of its creators and customers—not the expectations of speculative capital.* This is endurance thinking in practice.

Entrepreneurship as an endurance game requires a recalibration of what counts as progress. Vanity metrics—user downloads, social followers, media coverage—may create momentum in public perception, but they rarely reflect the quality of the business beneath. The better questions are: How resilient is your revenue? How much does your customer base trust you? How efficiently can you survive volatility? What have you learned about your market that others haven't? These are slow answers. They accumulate through iteration, not innovation theatre. But once earned, they compound like capital.

Part of this endurance ethic is recognising that *patience is not passivity.* It's active waiting—using time to gain insight, deepen advantage, and remove fragility. The founders who thrive over decades are constantly pruning distractions, refining their models, and reinvesting in fundamentals: product quality, employee culture, operational excellence. This doesn't make headlines, but it creates substance. Contrast this with startups that spend more time optimising pitch decks than their actual value propositions. The startup world is littered with companies that raised ten times what they needed and still failed—because they mistook access to capital for evidence of fit.

Another distinguishing feature of endurance entrepreneurship is the ability to operate without applause. During the "silent years"—those long stretches when no press is covering you, no investors are knocking, and no viral growth is happening—it's easy to assume you're on the wrong path. But these quiet phases are where the real advantages are forged. *They test your conviction, force you to focus, and reveal what you actually believe about your business.* The endurance entrepreneur learns to see these seasons not as failure, but as fermentation. Time becomes an ally, not a threat.

The psychological resilience required to sustain a company over decades is immense. Founders must learn to *say no more often than yes*, to resist the urge to chase every new opportunity, and to build in constraints that protect their time and focus. Endurance is about choosing hard things for longer than feels comfortable. It's not about getting lucky once—it's about remaining useful repeatedly. This philosophy also informs hiring, culture, and decision-making. Teams built for speed tend to optimise for stimulation; teams built for endurance optimise for reliability. One burns bright; the other lasts.

Importantly, the endurance mindset doesn't preclude ambition—it reframes it. Instead of asking "How big can we get, how fast?" it asks, "How useful can we become, how consistently?" This shift in orientation changes everything. It discourages gimmicks, hypes, and hollow marketing. It rewards reputation, resilience, and responsibility. In this context, profit is not just a financial outcome—it's a signal of alignment. It says, "We built something people value enough to pay for, and we did it sustainably."

This model of entrepreneurship also demands a different kind of financing. Traditional venture capital, with its expectations of 10x returns and aggressive growth timelines, often undermines the very durability it seeks to capitalise on. Endurance entrepreneurs are better served by patient capital: funding that values long-term stewardship over short-term liquidity. That may mean bootstrapping, working with aligned investors, or growing slower in order to stay in control. The goal is not to avoid risk, but to avoid *misaligned incentives*—because the wrong money can ruin the right business.

Endurance entrepreneurship is also more resilient to market cycles. During booms, it grows slowly but steadily. During downturns, it survives while over-leveraged competitors collapse. This isn't luck—it's preparation. Companies that have resisted overextension, built margin buffers, and maintained customer trust are far more likely to weather shocks. They can use downturns as opportunities to hire great people, gain market share, or deepen relationships with customers. *Resilience is not built in good times—it is revealed by them.*

Some of the most successful founders of our era embody this thinking, even when their public images suggest otherwise. Jeff Bezos, for all the growth of Amazon, maintained an unusually long time horizon for a public company. He repeatedly told investors to expect volatility and reinvestment. Warren Buffett built Berkshire Hathaway not by pursuing novelty but by understanding compounding and choosing disciplined operators. These are not flukes. They are *proofs of concept for enduring mental models.*

The takeaway is simple, but difficult to practise: entrepreneurship, if you intend to do it well, is a decades-long act of emotional patience and systems thinking. It is not a test of cleverness, but of clarity. Not a race for capital, but a craft of coherence. You are not building for the next investor memo—you are building for the next 25 years. And that requires a mindset capable of *quietly outlasting the noise.*

Those who play this game well rarely look like the fastest movers. But they often end up owning the terrain. Because they built when it was slow. They listened when others shouted. And they stayed when others left. Entrepreneurship is not about how you start. It's about how long you can stay useful—and how wisely you endure.

Saying No as a Wealth Strategy

Saying yes is easy. It flatters our ambition, signals open-mindedness, and feeds the illusion that more is always better—more connections, more opportunities, more exposure. But wealth, in its most sustainable and enduring forms, is often the consequence of deliberate subtraction. *Saying no is not about scarcity thinking; it is about strategic discipline.* It is the choice to preserve attention, protect compounding, and prioritise what truly matters over what merely looks attractive. In a world where distraction is monetised and urgency is weaponised, learning to say no—intelligently, consistently, and unapologetically—is not just a personal boundary. It's a long-term financial advantage.

The problem is that the modern professional environment, especially among high-achievers, is structured to reward responsiveness over restraint. Email inboxes are shaped like slot machines; social media platforms constantly signal new trends to chase; and career advice often over-indexes on networking, exposure, and hyper-productivity. Amid this noise, the person who pauses and declines—who filters rather than reacts—is often perceived as resistant or aloof. Yet, when viewed through the lens of wealth creation, that same restraint is often the very thing that protects optionality and fuels depth. *The ability to ignore 90% of available opportunities is what allows the remaining 10% to flourish fully.*

Warren Buffett once remarked, "The difference between successful people and really successful people is that really successful people say no to almost everything." This isn't just aphorism—it's operational philosophy. Buffett's investing style, famously long-term and minimalist, rests on the disciplined rejection of the majority of deals and ideas that come across his desk. While others chase market cycles, he waits. While others diversify prematurely, he concentrates. He has built generational wealth not by having more ideas, but by cultivating *a sharper filter for relevance, risk, and return.*

The wealth-building advantage of saying no is rooted in its compounding protection. Every unnecessary yes extracts a cost—be it cognitive bandwidth, financial capital, opportunity, or emotional energy. The person who habitually says yes dilutes their resources across too many fronts, introducing fragility into their career and capital. In contrast, someone who consistently rejects distractions can preserve energy for compounding efforts—those slow-building, high-yield activities like skill development, reputation refinement, or deep client trust. *What feels like patience is often just the discipline of not dispersing your focus.*

This is especially true in entrepreneurship, where founders are bombarded with partnerships, product pivots, platform experiments, and investor overtures. Saying yes to all of them is not strategic flexibility; it's brand erosion. Strong companies tend to have a clear identity not because they followed trends, but because they *refused most temptations to deviate from their vision.* Consider the case of In-N-Out Burger. While most fast-food chains expanded rapidly, diversified their menus, and chased marketing trends, In-N-Out focused obsessively on doing a few things extremely well—no franchises, no public ownership, no gimmicks. The result?

Remarkable margins, cult loyalty, and multi-generational ownership. Their "no" was more profitable than others' "yes."

Career trajectories benefit from the same logic. Early in one's professional life, it's tempting to adopt a philosophy of maximisation: go to every event, apply to every opportunity, explore every pivot. While exploration is valuable, unfiltered exposure becomes a trap. Each decision to pursue a shiny opportunity—be it a short-term role, a speculative project, or a trendy certification—delays the development of compounding expertise. The person who builds patiently—deepening their craft, reputation, and relationships in a chosen domain—will eventually command *asymmetric returns* that scattershot opportunists never reach.

This applies equally in academia, creative work, or corporate leadership. The scholar who writes fewer, better papers has more impact than the one who publishes endlessly without coherence. The artist who develops a singular style is remembered longer than the one who adapts endlessly to market tastes. The executive who declines non-essential meetings gains the mental bandwidth to make strategic decisions. *Concentration is what allows excellence to emerge; refusal is what allows concentration to persist.*

Saying no also inoculates against what might be called *reputational debt.* Every yes implicitly signals a commitment—to show up, to deliver, to endorse. As these accumulate, they create a burden. Not just in terms of time, but in terms of how others perceive your reliability. The person who commits promiscuously but delivers inconsistently is far less trusted than the one who *says no politely and follows through masterfully when they say yes.* Over time, a reputation for discernment becomes a competitive edge. It communicates quality control—not just in decision-making, but in self-awareness.

Financially, saying no protects from exposure to volatility you don't understand. The faddishness of speculative investment—whether in meme stocks, crypto surges, or short-lived tech IPOs—has cost many individuals dearly. These decisions are rarely made from careful analysis; they are emotional yeses, born from fear of missing out and fuelled by social proof. The emotionally patient investor, who can calmly say no to frenzy and wait for clarity, is not being timid. They are protecting a base that can compound undisturbed. *The wealthiest individuals are rarely those who took the most swings—they are those who protected their downside while waiting for the right pitch.*

There is also an ethical dimension to the strategy of refusal. To say no consistently, you must know what you value. You must decide what matters enough to deserve your time and capital. This clarity sharpens decision-making and anchors you during ambiguity. Saying no to lucrative but ethically questionable partnerships, for example, might cost short-term gain but builds *long-term credibility that becomes impossible to fake.* Clients, collaborators, and employees learn to trust you not just for your expertise, but for your *predictability under pressure.*

A common objection is that saying no can close doors or make one miss out on serendipitous opportunities. But this misunderstands how serendipity actually works. *Luck favours clarity.* The person with a defined direction attracts aligned opportunities. The person saying yes to everything diffuses their signal and becomes forgettable. Serendipity does not come from chasing everything; it comes from standing somewhere specific, long enough to be found.

There is, of course, a nuance to the practice of refusal. Saying no is not about arrogance, rigidity, or fear. It is about recognising that attention and energy are scarce resources. That every yes has a cost. That optionality only remains valuable if it's preserved, not spent frivolously. This means creating internal frameworks—questions, filters, principles—that guide when to engage and when to step aside. These systems protect from decision fatigue and preserve cognitive sharpness for what matters most.

Ultimately, saying no is an act of ownership. It affirms that *you, not your inbox, calendar, or social network, control your trajectory*. It is not an act of withdrawal—it is an act of intention. Wealth, in its enduring form, is the accumulation of well-directed time, trust, and talent. The person who masters the refusal of distraction will, in the long arc of time, outperform the person addicted to yes. Because behind every quiet "no" is a louder, longer "yes" to something that truly compounds.

In the end, the discipline to decline is not a suppression of ambition. It is its refinement. The professional who builds a career, a business, or a reputation on the backbone of thoughtful refusals creates not just wealth—but wisdom. They are not merely successful. They are sovereign.

Chapter 9
The Emotional Architecture of Legacy

Legacy is among the most overused, and perhaps most misunderstood, words in contemporary financial conversation. Too often it is reduced to a ledger exercise—what remains in portfolios, property, or endowments. Yet genuine legacy is not about the residue of wealth but the transfer of wisdom. The true durability of a family, an institution, or even a lineage depends less on the magnitude of its inheritance and more on the quality of its emotional scaffolding. What survives is not capital but character; not financial tactics, but temperament.

So the task begins with a reframing. When wealth is defined solely as money, it is already impoverished. Cash drains. Companies collapse. Trusts dissolve. But the ability to pause before acting, to remain composed under strain, to evaluate risk without succumbing to frenzy, to orient one's thinking in decades rather than in quarters—these are emotional competencies that persist, and, crucially, compound. Harder to quantify, yes, but far harder to erode. Legacy, when properly understood, is the bequest of resilience, moral clarity, and philosophical ballast. Everything else is mere accounting.

Any wealth plan that excludes emotional or behavioural training is a wager—a dangerous one. It presumes heirs will instinctively know how to manage what they receive. History is unsparing on this point: most family fortunes vanish within three generations. The cause is rarely a flaw in the legal scaffolding; it is a failure in emotional transmission. The values that created the wealth were not taught, not embedded, not lived. What was lost was not the money but the mindset.

This chapter, then, is not an inventory of estate instruments. It is an architecture of legacy thinking that places patience, decision-making stamina, and the weaving of trust across generations at its core. Earlier we considered how individuals can build financial durability through emotional discipline; here the harder question arises: can that discipline endure succession?

The premise is simple yet radical: emotional capital is real capital. Just as money compounds under careful stewardship, emotional strength can deepen—or deplete—over time. A family that trains its children to endure discomfort, to delay gratification, to resist the corrosive pull of comparison, builds an invisible reserve of power. This reservoir matters most when the inheritance itself produces volatility—whether in markets or in the very identities of those who inherit. The mark of a prepared successor is not wealth management, but coherence under turbulence.

Picture two families of equal net worth. The first reduces legacy to a technical procedure: trusts, tax minimisation, transfers. The second treats it as a developmental process: resilience is modelled, boundaries are taught, patience is practised, trade-offs are discussed openly. After two generations, their trajectories separate entirely. One leaves behind assets but breeds entitlement. The other, though exposed to inevitable setbacks, carries within it the capacity to rebuild, reinvest, and restore. One leaves heirs. The other produces stewards.

At the centre of this work is patience. Preaching prudence is inadequate without teaching the muscle memory that sustains it. Delayed gratification is not merely virtue-signalling—it is neurological conditioning, cultivated through example, story, and repeated practice. Recall the Stanford marshmallow test. It was never about sugar. It was about trust: did the child believe that the future would honour the promise of the present? Adults trained gradually in financial responsibility—permitted both to decide and to reflect—are far likelier to mature into disciplined allocators of capital.

But here lies a modern error: mistaking protection for preparation. Shielding heirs from discomfort or ambiguity may appear compassionate, but it breeds fragility. Wealth without psychological ballast destabilises more than it secures. To safeguard legacy, one must prepare the inheritor, not simply perfect the paperwork.

Indeed, the emotional climate of a family is its most decisive predictor of continuity. Do siblings trust one another? Can they disagree without detonating? Do they understand how choices are made and by whom? More importantly—do they grasp the values beneath the wealth, or only the structures that contain it? These are rarely broached in estate meetings, yet they quietly decide the fate of the plan. Conflict itself is not the enemy; unspoken, festering, inherited conflict is.

This is the territory of emotional inheritance. The aim is not to sanitise complexity, but to design mechanisms for dialogue, storytelling, and modelling. Legacy conversations held only in the shadow of death or legal triggers arrive too late. The real transmission occurs in everyday moments—crises endured, victories marked, choices observed. Children remember less of what is said and more of how decisions were embodied under stress.

It is vital, too, to distinguish principles from tactics. Tax strategies, equity structures, debt manoeuvres—all have their place. Yet they are transient, swept aside by shifting laws or markets. Principles, however—clarity of values, patience in compounding, humility before risk—outlast those changes. Families that root education in principles rather than tactics create a coherence that survives disruption.

The evidence is plain in families and enterprises that have endured for centuries. What unites them is not size, nor necessarily brilliance, but alignment. Alignment between stated values, lived behaviour, structures, and collective purpose. This alignment is emotional. It binds members to a shared sense of what wealth is for. When that answer is clear—when wealth is framed as stewardship rather than status—longevity follows. When it is absent, fracture ensues.

Here enters the notion of purposeful wealth. Wealth untethered from purpose drifts into envy, aimlessness, or malaise. Wealth linked to service, learning, or shared aspiration, by contrast, coheres. Legacy, therefore, cannot be about what is handed down alone, but why it is handed down. To fund learning? To underwrite risk? To preserve memory? To support others? Clarity of intention dissolves much of the conflict that transitions otherwise ignite.

No chapter can promise a conflict-free inheritance. Emotional literacy is not a magic seal. But observation suggests it is a far stronger predictor of continuity than technical precision alone.

Legacy stripped to finance misses its essence. What compounds across generations is rarely money. It is the discipline of decisions made consistently, values lived openly, relationships tended deliberately.

In the pages ahead, we will consider the core dimensions of emotional legacy: the training of patience, the modelling of judgement, the crafting of dialogue, the codification of principle. Not only the successes, but the failures too—the well-meaning strategies that unravel when emotional foundations are absent. We will look at how families, institutions, and individuals can construct systems that transmit wisdom rather than merely wealth.

If earlier we treated patience as an individual superpower, here its highest expression comes into view: generational patience. The courage to plant seeds whose shade one may never sit beneath. That is legacy. Not a number on a balance sheet, but a stance, a discipline, an architecture. Built carefully, it survives the builder.

Wealth Beyond Money

Wealth, as it is most commonly understood, is too narrow a term to describe what the wisest individuals and families truly hope to pass on. Bank balances, equity stakes, property portfolios—these are useful instruments, but they are not the essence of legacy. They are transient, inherently exposed to decay, market volatility, poor management, or the entropy of time. What endures across generations is not the currency of finance, but the *currency of character*. Emotional resilience, decision-making discipline, philosophical clarity—these are forms of wealth that do not show up on spreadsheets but define whether inherited resources become seeds or burdens.

The assumption that financial assets automatically translate into prosperity is not only wrong—it is dangerous. In countless examples, we see fortunes disintegrate not because of external shocks, but because the inheritors lacked the emotional infrastructure to steward their windfall. What was missing wasn't information. It was *identity*. Without a core sense of purpose, values, and patience, wealth confuses more than it empowers. When money arrives faster than maturity, the result is not progress—it is erosion.

To redefine legacy as *emotional wealth* is to elevate the parts of a life that cannot be transferred through legal documents but are deeply transferable through example, conversation, and culture. These include how one responds to stress, how one interprets failure, how one frames ambition, how one makes trade-offs, how one thinks across timescales longer than a quarterly earnings report. These are teachable, but only to those willing to see that the most powerful inheritance is *behavioural, not transactional.*

Consider families that have preserved not just capital, but coherence, across three or more generations. You'll find they talk differently. They do not just discuss market trends or estate structures; they speak about decision thresholds, personal restraint, mutual responsibility, and long arcs of purpose. Their dinner table conversations are not driven by quarterly gains but by long-term stewardship. Their language contains emotional signal: trust, sacrifice, patience, identity, consequence. It is these conversations—not asset allocations—that form the bedrock of true multigenerational wealth.

This is not to dismiss the importance of financial education. On the contrary, understanding money mechanics—taxes, investment strategy, compounding, debt—matters deeply. But it must be grounded in a psychological frame. A technically informed child without emotional maturity is simply a more efficient spender. Knowledge alone does not produce wisdom. *It is the integration of knowledge with values, restraint, and long-term thinking that creates financial adults from financial dependents.*

The emotional assets that deserve to be transferred—grit, patience, discernment, tolerance for ambiguity—are not accidental by-products of growing up in a wealthy household. They must be consciously cultivated. And they are best transmitted not through instruction, but through modelling. When children witness adults confronting uncertainty without panic, deferring gratification without complaint, maintaining integrity under pressure—they absorb these patterns far more deeply than they do from any seminar or financial planning app.

This is why legacy planning must begin decades before any transfer of wealth occurs. It is not a retirement activity; it is a parenting philosophy, a leadership practice, a worldview. It means building a culture where *how* decisions are made is discussed as openly as *what* decisions are made. It requires that families reflect not only on their assets, but on their principles—and even more so, on how well those principles are known, shared, and practised.

Some families create family constitutions or charters to articulate these values. Others rely on stories, rituals, and traditions. The medium matters less than the consistency and depth of engagement. A set of investment guidelines written on paper but never discussed is meaningless. A story told every year at a family gathering about how the founder overcame hardship by thinking long-term is likely to have far more behavioural influence. *Narrative, not instruction, often determines cultural transmission.*

A crucial part of emotional legacy is preparing heirs not for wealth, but for volatility. The world into which they will step is not the world their parents navigated. Markets will fluctuate, industries will collapse, careers will become non-linear, and public trust in institutions may further erode. To prepare someone for this landscape means giving them the internal tools to adapt without losing their values. This includes teaching them how to hold two ideas in tension: optimism and realism, ambition and patience, agency and humility.

Resilience here does not mean stubbornness. It means the capacity to bend without breaking. This is a deeply undervalued form of wealth. When emotional resilience is high, people take appropriate risks, endure setbacks without meltdown, and preserve optionality even in constrained conditions. When it is low, even abundance leads to collapse—through burnout, panic decisions, or interpersonal conflict. It is no coincidence that studies of long-term family wealth retention cite *communication, trust, and shared purpose*—not market performance—as the most critical factors for continuity.

Philosophical wealth is equally overlooked. What does this family believe money is *for*? Is it a vehicle for comfort, power, contribution, exploration, safety, legacy? The answer to this question shapes every downstream decision. If the purpose of wealth is never examined, it will default to the values of the loudest voice in the room—or worse, the cultural noise of the moment. Families that do not align on purpose often implode under the weight of ambiguous expectations.

It's worth noting that some of the world's most intentional philanthropists and builders have taken this idea seriously. Warren Buffett, despite his enormous fortune, has famously said he wishes to leave his children "enough to do anything, but not enough to do nothing." That sentiment reflects a deep philosophical stance: wealth should be empowering but not entitling. This subtle distinction is at the heart of healthy legacy building. It assumes *agency is the goal—not insulation.*

Other examples are more private but equally powerful. Consider the families that require heirs to work in public service, operate in different industries, or meet educational and behavioural milestones before accessing certain funds. While these may be contractual obligations, the underlying message is philosophical: wealth is earned through responsibility, not simply passed on like a birthright. It is to be used with discretion and accountability—not as a substitute for personal development.

The challenge, of course, is that emotional and philosophical assets are harder to quantify. They do not appear on wealth reports or tax returns. They are not insurable. But they are profoundly measurable in outcome: Does the next generation feel a sense of purpose? Do they make high-quality decisions under pressure? Do they collaborate or fragment? Do they grow the wealth, redefine it, or squander it? The answers to these questions reflect not what was written in the will, but what was *lived in the household.*

Ultimately, redefining wealth as emotional and philosophical resilience is not a rejection of financial capital—it is an elevation of its purpose. It is an understanding that money, when paired with maturity, becomes a lever. Without maturity, it becomes a weight. The goal is not simply to grow assets, but to *grow people*—people who can think independently, decide wisely, absorb adversity, and stay anchored to values larger than themselves.

Legacy, in this light, is not the conclusion of a financial plan. It is the embodiment of a lived philosophy, transferred not in one moment but across many conversations, decisions, and silences. To leave true wealth is to have spent years *becoming the kind of person whose example is more valuable than their assets*. That is wealth beyond money. That is what endures.

Teaching Patience to the Next Generation

The child who can wait has a competitive advantage that no inheritance can replicate. Patience—more precisely, emotional patience—is a foundational capability that determines not only future financial outcomes, but also the resilience, confidence, and agency with which a young person engages the world. Unlike technical skills, which can be taught and forgotten, emotional patience embeds itself into the nervous system through lived experience. It governs how discomfort is processed, how desire is managed, how setbacks are interpreted. And yet, while most parents or educators would agree it's important, few treat it as a skill that can be deliberately cultivated. Fewer still know how.

The challenge is not that modern children are inherently less patient; it's that they are being raised in an environment meticulously engineered to undermine patience. From instant streaming to gamified apps to one-click gratification, the ambient message is clear: faster is better, now is optimal, friction is failure. Under these conditions, patience does not develop organically. It must be designed into the child's environment with the same rigour we apply to diet, education, or safety. *Teaching patience, then, is not about moral lectures—it is about psychological architecture.*

The most instructive entry point remains the now-famous "Marshmallow Test," first conducted by Walter Mischel at Stanford in the 1970s. In this experiment, children were given a simple choice: eat one marshmallow now, or wait 15 minutes and receive two. Follow-up studies tracked these participants for decades and found striking correlations: those who had the ability to delay gratification performed better in academic achievement, health outcomes, income, and stress management. While the original findings have since been nuanced by further research—including the role of trust, environment, and socio-economic background—the core insight remains intact: *the ability to wait is predictive of long-term flourishing.*

But knowing this is not the same as knowing what to do about it. Parents and mentors are often tempted to approach emotional patience as a trait to be commanded: "Be patient." "Calm down." "Just wait your turn." These are not instructions; they are wishful thinking. The child does not have the circuitry yet. Patience is not the suppression of desire—it is the intelligent navigation of it. And that navigation must be learned through structured, emotionally safe practice.

The most powerful method is *graduated delay*. Start with scenarios in which the child is required to wait just slightly longer than feels comfortable—but not so long that the wait becomes punitive. This could be as simple as serving dessert five minutes after the meal, or setting a rule that new toys are bought only after a one-week cooling period. What matters is that the child begins to associate waiting not with deprivation, but with clarity and satisfaction. With time, the intervals can increase. The emotional system, like a muscle, adapts to greater loads through repetition.

Critically, delayed gratification must come with consistent feedback loops. The payoff should be visible, tangible, and framed in language the child can internalise: "You waited, and now you're enjoying the extra story because you used your time well." Over time, this builds not only patience, but *self-efficacy*—the belief that one can shape outcomes through restraint and intention.

Equally essential is modelling. If adults in a child's life react to frustration with impatience—if they demand instant responses, multi-task compulsively, or treat waiting as a flaw—they should not be surprised when children replicate that tempo. Children are not told what to become; they observe it. If a parent delays a purchase to research it further, takes time to calm before reacting, or saves visibly for something meaningful, those cues carry far more instructional weight than any verbal advice. *Emotional patience is most effectively transmitted through observation, not lecture.*

Technology presents a particularly thorny challenge. Devices provide a constant drip-feed of novelty, a dopamine-rich environment that makes ordinary waiting feel intolerable. While banning screens altogether is rarely practical, recalibrating their use is essential. One strategy is to introduce digital "speed bumps": download delays, scheduled viewing times, or usage tied to non-digital tasks. Another is to expose children to longer-form media—books, documentaries, in-depth games—that reward attention rather than fragment it. *The goal is not to reject technology, but to reorient it from immediacy to engagement.*

It is also vital to differentiate between forced patience and chosen patience. When a child is made to wait against their will, without context or control, they learn helplessness. But when they are invited into a system of cause and effect—where waiting yields enhanced rewards, greater autonomy, or higher trust—they learn agency. This is the psychological leap from compliance to maturity. *True patience is not passive—it is strategic.*

There is also a deeper layer to this discussion, one that reaches beyond parenting into cultural design. Western economies often valorise speed, ambition, and hyper-competence. Childhood is increasingly structured around accelerated learning, early achievement, and precocious performance. In this context, patience can appear synonymous with passivity or falling behind. But this view is short-sighted. The highest performers across disciplines—from elite athletes to long-term investors—routinely exhibit *delayed gratification, long-term orientation, and emotional endurance.* To teach children patience is not to suppress ambition—it is to equip them to pace it.

This brings us to another powerful technique: *decision reflection.* After a child has made a choice—especially one involving trade-offs or delay—invite them to talk about how they made that decision. Ask questions like, "Was it hard to wait?", "How did you feel while you were deciding?", or "Would you do it the same way next time?" These questions aren't about right or wrong; they are about building *meta-cognition*—the ability to think about one's own thinking. This level of reflection trains emotional intelligence and strengthens the neural pathways associated with long-term reasoning.

One of the most underused tools in cultivating patience is boredom. In a world oversaturated with stimuli, boredom is often treated as a problem to be solved. But boredom is the birthplace of creativity, self-regulation, and curiosity. Children who are occasionally left to entertain themselves—without screens, scheduled activities, or immediate gratification—develop internal resources. They learn to sit with discomfort, to explore, to invent. These are the muscles that support lifelong resilience. *Boredom, handled correctly, is a developmental asset—not a deficiency.*

Teaching patience also requires a redefinition of progress. Progress in emotional development is rarely linear or externally visible. There will be regressions, tantrums, complaints. That does not mean the system is failing. It means the child is in training. Like any skill-building process, the path to emotional maturity involves cycles of success, challenge, and consolidation. The key is consistency, not perfection.

Families who successfully transmit emotional patience across generations often do so by embedding it into their narratives. They talk about ancestors who built slowly, endured hardship, and made long-term choices. They praise restraint as much as achievement. They normalise waiting, ambiguity, and effort. These families do not confuse comfort with growth. They understand that *emotional strength is not inherited—it is practised.*

Lastly, patience should not be treated as an isolated skill but as part of a broader framework of emotional literacy. Teach children to recognise their emotions, label them accurately, and understand how feelings influence behaviour. When a child knows they are feeling anxious, impatient, or overstimulated, they can begin to make decisions with greater awareness. The ability to *pause before acting* is the highest form of behavioural maturity—and it starts with self-recognition.

In summary, cultivating patience in children is not a passive hope but an active discipline. It requires thoughtful design, emotional modelling, and deliberate practice. It is one of the rare investments that pays off across every domain of life—financial, relational, intellectual, and personal. And it is the foundation upon which every other virtue can be built. To teach patience is to future-proof a mind. It is to equip the next generation with the capacity to think beyond the moment and act from strength rather than impulse. That is not merely parenting. That is leadership.

The Transfer of Emotional Capital

It is no exaggeration to say that the majority of inherited wealth does not survive the third generation. This pattern—observed across dynasties, industries, and borders—is often simplistically attributed to irresponsible heirs or poor estate planning. But that diagnosis misses the deeper cause. Families fail not because they run out of money, but because they run out of meaning. *Emotional capital—the shared values, resilience, identity, and relational trust that undergird wealth—is often more perishable than financial capital.* When families misunderstand this, they devote disproportionate effort to transferring assets and insufficient energy to transferring wisdom. What endures over generations is rarely money. It is mindset.

In financial discourse, we speak comfortably of compounding interest, asset allocation, and fiduciary duty. Yet emotional capital—equally foundational—is seldom addressed in formal wealth discussions, despite being the substrate on which sustainable legacies are built. It is invisible in spreadsheets, absent from tax codes, and underappreciated by many advisors. But families that ignore it do so at their peril. Wealth without emotional stewardship is unstable; it amplifies dysfunction and often accelerates disintegration. The true challenge of intergenerational wealth is not how to preserve money—it is how to preserve meaning.

One of the most underrecognised forces in this arena is *intergenerational emotional modelling.* Parents and grandparents do not merely pass down principles through instruction—they transmit them through behaviour. How a parent reacts to loss, handles ambiguity, speaks about money, or navigates success—all of this quietly informs a child's mental model for adulthood. Families that inadvertently teach fear, entitlement, or scarcity leave behind a far more corrosive inheritance than poor asset selection ever could. *Children absorb emotional cues long before they inherit financial statements.*

A particularly revealing example is how families handle financial setbacks. When a family experiences business loss, litigation, or market downturn, the emotional tone of their response becomes a crucial pedagogical moment. Do they treat it as shameful failure, breeding secrecy and blame? Or as a temporary trial to be faced with transparency, reflection, and growth? These responses teach far more than lectures. They define the household's emotional vocabulary—its tolerance for vulnerability, its openness to risk, and its clarity about what truly matters. *Emotional capital is built most reliably not during triumph, but in how a family metabolises difficulty.*

Another powerful dynamic is the *narrative architecture* of a family—the stories it tells about itself. Some families pass down myths of sacrifice, grit, and contribution; others perpetuate tales of entitlement or persecution. These narratives function like internal scripts that shape identity and behaviour. Children raised on stories of perseverance are more likely to see struggle as normal and worthwhile. Those raised on narratives of exceptionalism may conflate self-worth with superiority and entitlement. Over time, these mental models influence everything from career ambition to risk appetite to generosity. *The healthiest legacies are not built on money alone, but on stories that anchor identity to purpose rather than privilege.*

This underscores a difficult truth: *wealth transfer is not neutral.* Money amplifies pre-existing emotional structures. A healthy family may find that inheritance reinforces shared goals and strengthens bonds. A fractured family, by contrast, may find that money accelerates mistrust, rivalry, or estrangement. Estate plans, no matter how elegantly drafted, cannot manufacture emotional maturity. That has to be cultivated deliberately and early, well before wills and trusts are signed. The real preparation for inheritance is not legal but psychological: *how well have the inheritors been equipped to carry not just assets, but meaning, responsibility, and discernment?*

Some of the most enduring multigenerational families treat wealth as stewardship rather than possession. They hold regular family meetings not just to review investments, but to debate values. They invite children into philanthropic decision-making to develop empathy and responsibility. They articulate family missions that transcend any one person's financial interests. Crucially, they normalise dissent, allow for individual paths, and invest in relationships outside the financial sphere. *They understand that emotional coherence cannot be decreed—it must be co-created.*

Contrast this with families who treat money as taboo. In such households, children grow up financially illiterate yet emotionally loaded—fearing that talking about money is greedy, or worse, that love is conditional upon financial success. In others, money is discussed constantly but used manipulatively—as a tool to control behaviour or signal status. Neither extreme fosters emotional capital. *True wealth literacy involves both technical competence and emotional clarity—a capacity to talk about money without letting it dominate identity or distort relationships.*

We also see patterns in *inter-sibling dynamics* within high-net-worth families. Where emotional capital is weak, money becomes a proxy for fairness, validation, or competition. Adult siblings may feud over minor allocations because deeper issues—recognition, autonomy, worth—were never addressed. But in families where trust and communication are nurtured early, financial outcomes are often secondary. These families understand that *no distribution formula can compensate for decades of unspoken resentment.* Investing in emotional literacy, empathy, and shared meaning is not a "soft skill" but a structural safeguard for preserving cohesion.

One might ask: how does one measure or build emotional capital in a meaningful, tangible way? While it resists quantification, there are observable indicators. Families with high emotional capital typically demonstrate:

– A shared language for discussing money and meaning, without avoidance or over-identification
– Regular, intergenerational dialogues grounded in listening, not hierarchy

– Openness to emotional diversity, without needing everyone to conform to one view of success
– Resilience in the face of uncertainty, built through narrative reflection and value clarity
– Intentional rituals—giving, mentorship, storytelling—that reinforce identity across generations

All of this takes time. There is no shortcut, no single seminar that implants emotional intelligence. It is built in micro-moments: the way a parent debriefs a mistake, the questions asked at dinner, the tone of voice when talking about others' success. It is taught through observation, repetition, and trust. And like compound interest, its effects are invisible at first but profound over time.

Philosophically, this invites a radical reframing of legacy. If wealth is defined as capital that produces generative outcomes, then *emotional capital may be the most valuable asset a family can steward.* It produces not only financial continuity, but also psychological safety, ethical reflection, and the capacity to make long-term decisions amidst complexity. A family with modest financial resources but strong emotional capital may thrive across generations. A wealthy family with weak emotional infrastructure is often fragile despite appearances.

Ultimately, the question families must grapple with is not "How much are we leaving?" but "What are we leaving behind?" Are we transferring tools or burdens, values or vacuums, clarity or confusion? Do our heirs inherit a map—or just a vault?

To build legacy worthy of its name, families must elevate emotional capital from an afterthought to a strategic imperative. Because what is remembered—what shapes lives—is rarely the net worth. It is the *framework for making sense of it.*

Enduring Principles Over Temporary Tactics

There is a quiet arrogance that runs through much of modern wealth management: the belief that strategy is king, and that timely tactics—well-executed, cleverly engineered—can outmanoeuvre uncertainty.

In truth, tactics are fragile. They expire. They respond to trends, chase optimisation, and often deliver a false sense of security. Over time, the advantage of tactics erodes, especially when untethered from a coherent foundation. *Enduring wealth, by contrast, is governed not by tactics but by principles.* The families, businesses, and individuals who build legacies that last do not merely adopt clever strategies—they operate from a deeply internalised code. That code is their compass through volatility.

When values-based planning is dismissed as "soft" or "philosophical", it reflects a fundamental misunderstanding of how complex systems behave over time. Financial markets, businesses, and families are not machines to be controlled—they are ecosystems to be navigated. In ecosystems, feedback loops, adaptation, and long-term coherence matter more than short-term precision. A well-formed principle—resilience, discipline, stewardship, patience—performs reliably across market cycles. Tactics, however brilliant, often collapse under stress or become obsolete. *It is principle that endures beyond context.*

Consider how different investors responded to the 2008 financial crisis. Some attempted tactical pivots: pulling out of equities, shifting to gold, trying to call the bottom. A few got lucky. Most locked in permanent losses or whipsawed themselves into paralysis. But those who had anchored their portfolios to principles—diversification, long time horizons, tolerance for drawdowns—fared better. They didn't need to guess. They didn't need to react. *Principles immunise you from the tyranny of reaction.* Over a career, over a generation, this difference compounds dramatically.

The same logic applies to family enterprises. It is common to see wealthy families seek the "best" legal structure, investment strategy, or governance model—often copied from peers or sold by consultants. Yet families are not spreadsheets. What sustains them is not the architecture of their trust documents but the alignment of their decisions with shared beliefs. A family that has clarified its commitment to integrity, contribution, and prudence will make very different investment and succession decisions than one operating reactively or egoically. *Wealth preservation without values is merely inertia.*

One telling example is the Walton family, heirs to the Walmart fortune. Despite extraordinary wealth, the family has remained notably understated, long-term oriented, and disciplined in governance. Their investment vehicles have avoided speculative fads, their public exposure is measured, and their philanthropic commitments have focused on education and community development—areas consistent with Sam Walton's original ethos. These are not tactical decisions—they are principle-led expressions of identity. That coherence acts as ballast across generations.

Contrast this with the collapse of once-prominent dynasties who, flush with cash, pursued trend-driven ventures, ostentatious consumption, or internecine legal battles. Their downfall was not due to inadequate strategy but incoherent identity. Money without philosophy is combustible. Without unifying values, even the best tactics create division, confusion, and drift. *Values provide the connective tissue across decisions, generations, and unpredictable futures.*

There is also a psychological dimension to values-based planning that is routinely undervalued: *clarity reduces anxiety*. People often over-optimise because they are uncertain about what matters. In financial contexts, this leads to excessive trading, compulsive tax avoidance, or overengineered estate plans. But when individuals or families have articulated what they stand for—what constitutes "enough," what goals are non-negotiable, what trade-offs are acceptable—they are liberated from the need to react to every fluctuation. *A principle-led life is calmer, because it is directional.*

To be clear, principles are not vague platitudes. They must be defined, stress-tested, and operationalised. "Integrity" means little until it dictates how one behaves under pressure. "Stewardship" becomes real when it shapes a budget or a hiring decision. Effective families and investors *translate values into rules of thumb*, such as: "We will not invest in ventures that exploit short-term leverage for cosmetic growth," or "Philanthropy will focus on efforts that build self-sufficiency rather than dependency." These aren't strategies; they are boundary conditions that guide strategy.

There is also a competitive advantage embedded in values. Because most actors in the financial or entrepreneurial ecosystem are optimising for quarterly results or next-year returns, long-term, principle-aligned behaviour often looks irrational in the short run. That appearance is deceptive. *What seems like underperformance is often deferred compounding.* Berkshire Hathaway's refusal to chase fashionable investments often attracted ridicule—until decades of steady performance and capital preservation proved the wisdom of its posture. Its underlying value system—rationality, patience, integrity—was not a tactic. It was a worldview.

The institutional investment world has begun to acknowledge this. Endowments with long time horizons—such as those of Harvard, Yale, or the Church of England—have often outperformed by adhering to values of asset-class diversification, downside protection, and long-term stewardship, even when these looked conservative relative to market highs. When asked why they held unglamorous positions or illiquid assets, these institutions often cite mission alignment and philosophical clarity—not tactical arbitrage. Their discipline reflects the maturity of principle over the seduction of trend.

Within business itself, founders who build enduring enterprises tend to hold a consistent set of values even as they adapt their strategies. Patagonia, for instance, has reshaped its product lines, technology, and marketing tactics over the decades—but its commitment to environmental responsibility, employee dignity, and ethical sourcing has never wavered. These principles serve not as constraints but as strategic filters. *Values simplify decision-making under uncertainty.* They provide consistency without rigidity.

Families that treat values as cosmetic or ceremonial pay a steep price when crises arise. They often discover that they are not aligned on core questions: Should we prioritise capital growth or stability? Is it more important to fund private education or generational philanthropy? How much autonomy should each family member have in making financial decisions? Without shared answers to these, trust erodes. Tactical disagreements become personal. Even well-meaning planning becomes performative. *Values-based planning is the only way to avoid these slow fractures.*

This is not to say tactics don't matter. They do—but only in service of principles. The key is sequencing: principles first, then tactics. Strategy flows downstream from worldview. If the worldview is confused or incoherent, no amount of technical brilliance will compensate. Conversely, when the worldview is clear, even imperfect tactics can deliver excellent outcomes over time. *The power lies not in perfection but in persistence of purpose.*

Ultimately, values-based planning is not a retreat from rigour—it is its deepest expression. It requires asking questions that most financial frameworks avoid: What is this money for? What kind of people do we hope to become? What do we want to be remembered for? These are not distractions from financial planning—they are its foundation. Without them, even the most sophisticated plan is vulnerable to misalignment, conflict, and drift. With them, the plan becomes a living expression of meaning.

In the end, wealth that endures is not merely protected—it is *directed.* It moves through time not as a static inheritance, but as a moral and practical force aligned with its originators' values. This requires more than legal skill. It requires philosophical clarity, emotional maturity, and intergenerational coherence. Families who commit to this work often find that the wealth they preserve is not just financial—it is relational, reputational, and deeply human. *Because when tactics fail—and they always do, eventually—principles remain.*

Conclusion
The Quiet Power to Outlast

The sharpest edge in any field is almost invisible. It isn't speed, nor clever tactics, nor privileged access. It is emotional patience—the quiet capacity to remain steady, to hold course, and to make considered choices under pressure for longer than others can tolerate. This has been the undertone running through every chapter of this book, less as pep talk than as strategy. Here, at the end, it must be pulled into the light. Not as a coda, but as the organising thesis: in an age enthralled by speed, the most underestimated wealth is endurance.

To endure is to excel, though not in the short-term sense so often paraded by markets and media. It means surviving volatility, resisting temptations, absorbing doubt, and holding faith long enough for compounding—of money, skill, reputation, relationships—to work its invisible magic. This posture is not passive, not resignation. It is a choice to exercise discipline precisely when uncertainty demands reaction. And the record is clear: the finest investors, the most resilient founders, the creators who last are defined not by their models or hacks, but by their temperament. They stayed—and in staying, they separated.

But data alone is insufficient. The deeper claim of this book is that patience is not just effective. It is transformative. Practised long enough, it alters our relationship with time, labour, risk, even identity. It quietly reshapes our philosophy: from "What can I seize now?" to "What is worth building slowly?" From "How do I keep up?" to "What deserves my constancy?" From "How can I win?" to "Who am I becoming?"

This reorientation is anything but small. It demands an internal rewiring, a rebellion against the twitch-reflexes of modern culture. It is a return to older, harder virtues—restraint, humility, endurance, clarity. These are not qualities society happens to drill into us; they are ones we must cultivate, intentionally, daily, against the noise. And so the closing ambition of this work is to offer not only intellectual casework for patience, but an architecture by which it becomes lived.

Consider what patience protects. It shields us from our own worst impulses: panic selling, social comparison, overreach, flinching at discomfort. It grants room to breathe. It creates distance from urgency. It allows us to move at the pace of meaning. Patience is not passivity. It is restraint with teeth. It is the discipline to withhold when intervention is premature. It is the clarity to delay when the world clamours for haste. It is wisdom acquired only through repeated practice.

The irony is sharp: while patience feels like slowing down, it is in truth how time is accelerated in our favour. Capital, trust, credibility—none can be hurried without fragility. Attempts to force them collapse under their own acceleration. Those who learn to wait with intelligence, to inhabit discomfort without panic, eventually gain a form of asymmetry others cannot: compounding that arrives slowly, then suddenly.

Across these pages we have dismantled the cult of speed, showing that intensity and proximity are not the levers of endurance. But the lesson cuts deeper: it is not pace but posture that matters. The posture of patience says: I do not chase, because what matters cannot be stolen. I do not scramble to prove, because time does the proving. I do not gamble on prediction, because principles will suffice. From such a stance, better decisions emerge—not flawless, but grounded.

And so we close with a question, posed not for rhetoric but for reflection: Who might you become if you truly learned to wait well? Not passively. Not indefinitely. But with structure, dignity, and resolve. Could you resist the endless churn of financial media? Could you decline the envy of premature wins? Could you persist at the unglamorous work—the saving, the training, the parenting, the building—long before recognition arrives?

Few will. The pull of immediacy is too strong, the reward of restraint too delayed. Yet those who manage it will find themselves standing when others have long burned out. They will own the assets that compound quietly, reputations that don't need repairing, relationships that deepen rather than splinter. They will not waste themselves in distraction or reinvention. And most of all, they will possess an internal wealth that eludes measurement: a calm trust in their own process.

To ground this, the book closes with practice. An emotional wealth discipline—simple, repeatable, imperfect, yet durable. No gimmicks, no checklists masquerading as answers. One hour each week in reflective writing. Ten minutes daily of deliberate stillness. A monthly review of commitments that extend years ahead. A quarterly pause to ask whether actions align with declared purpose. Practised unevenly, even clumsily, these rituals become a kind of scaffolding. They render patience visible.

Just as physical strength is built not from inspiration but from repeated exertion, emotional strength—the kind behind resilient investing, parenting, entrepreneurship—comes not from ideas but from integration. Rituals, not theories. Practices, not platitudes. Once embedded, the transformation is not cosmetic. It is structural.

Remember the stakes. In markets, patience is the only edge that doesn't erode. In careers, the only signal that outlasts noise. In family, the only inheritance immune to loss. In leadership, the only power that doesn't corrode. And in life itself, the only ground from which wisdom flowers. That is the quiet power with which we conclude—not because it dazzles, but because it endures.

We live in a world that idolises motion, but it is stillness that compounds. We are urged to chase, but it is restraint that preserves. We are taught to win fast, but it is those who endure who shape what remains. That is your invitation. Not to sprint harder, but to stand steadier. Not to react faster, but to decide with care. Not to outshine, but to outlast. Everything else follows.

The Hidden Wealth of Calm Endurance

If there is a single discipline that unifies the greatest investors, founders, creators, and decision-makers across history, it is not brilliance, access, or even opportunity. It is the capacity to *endure without panic.* Quietly, consistently, often invisibly, emotional patience outperforms brilliance when brilliance cannot sit still. In a world addicted to speed, noise, and immediacy, the calm mind is not merely rare—it is radically undervalued. This is the hidden wealth of calm endurance: not a soft virtue, but a strategic, economic, and psychological advantage that compounds in ways markets and metrics often fail to capture.

This book has offered evidence, case studies, and frameworks to support one central argument: *emotional patience is not merely an edge—it is a revolution in how we think about wealth.* It shifts the axis of decision-making from short-term optimisation to long-term orientation. It refuses to play the frantic game of predictions, and instead cultivates a temperament fit for compounding, resilience, and optionality. It is neither passive nor naïve. It is active resistance to distraction, distortion, and urgency. To call this a mindset is accurate, but insufficient. It is a discipline—practised, tested, sharpened over time. And it changes everything.

Consider the performance of long-term investors who do less, not more. In study after study, retail investors who trade frequently underperform not just benchmarks, but even inflation-adjusted savings accounts. The reason is not lack of intelligence. It is emotional interference: impatience, overconfidence, herd behaviour, and fear. Meanwhile, investors like Warren Buffett and Charlie Munger—whose portfolios are built not on forecasts but on the capacity to *wait well*—consistently outpace peers. The power is not in their models. It is in their *ability to endure the boredom of compounding* without flinching.

The same principle applies in business. Companies that chase short-term earnings, quarterly targets, and news-driven strategy often burn out their margins—and their people. Contrast that with organisations built on enduring principles, deliberate strategy, and founder patience. Patagonia, for instance, made long-term ecological commitments decades before sustainability was fashionable. It didn't pivot to trends—it stayed anchored in purpose. That calm posture has yielded not just brand trust, but lasting value. It is not the speed of adaptation, but the clarity of non-reaction that protected it.

This kind of calm endurance is not intuitive. The modern economy rewards spectacle. Media cycles amplify drama. Social platforms gamify visibility. Every incentive points toward motion. But what outlasts the noise is never the fastest mover—it is the *most stable architecture*. This is true of portfolios, companies, careers, and families. Endurance becomes wealth not because it moves first, but because it stays longest. It builds slowly what cannot be built quickly: trust, insight, credibility, capacity, clarity.

What makes calm endurance so powerful is not that it avoids risk—but that it *stays composed through risk*. It doesn't require certainty. It tolerates ambiguity. This is where emotional patience distinguishes itself from generic optimism. Patience is not wishful thinking. It is disciplined conviction in the presence of discomfort. It allows us to hold positions others would exit, maintain values others would compromise, and build strategies others would rush. And it makes us—quietly but unambiguously—stronger than volatility.

Psychologists often describe patience as a form of emotional regulation, a temperamental trait. But this underestimates its developmental nature. Patience can be trained. It can be designed into systems. It can be scaffolded by environment. In investing, that means automatic contributions, pre-committed allocation, and rules that override mood. In business, that means mission-based frameworks, long-term KPIs, and governance that protects against overreaction. In parenting and teaching, it means structure, space, and principled repetition. Across domains, patience can be embedded *intentionally*, not hoped for.

Yet this discipline comes at a psychological cost. To practise calm endurance is to often look wrong in the short term. It requires resisting the social validation of movement. It asks us to forego the dopamine of updates, the thrill of pivots, and the applause of fast wins. This is why most people abandon it. They mistake noise for momentum. They assume quiet means weakness. But over time, the signal separates from the noise. The emotional investor who sat still beats the active trader who tried to time every tremor. The entrepreneur who refused to chase fads owns a brand. The individual who declined distractions holds compound clarity. *The reward for endurance is not just survival—it is separation.*

This perspective demands a reframing of what it means to be "wealthy." Traditional wealth is defined financially—assets under management, net worth, income. But these markers often ignore volatility, fragility, and emotional cost. A trader who earns 20% a year but lives in panic is not wealthy. A founder whose valuation spikes but sleeps four hours a night is not wealthy. A professional who earns prestige but feels brittle, reactive, and hollow is not wealthy. Real wealth is the *capacity to sustain high-quality decisions under pressure, without being emotionally hijacked.* That is what calm endurance enables.

There is, of course, a cultural component to this revolution in wealth thinking. Much of what we admire in traditional success—speed, hustle, risk-taking—is performative. It signals energy. But calm does not signal. It builds. It is less visible because it is internal. That makes it harder to celebrate, but more essential to protect. And as volatility increases—whether economic, political, or technological—the value of those who can *remain rational while others unravel* will rise. Calm becomes not just a virtue, but a moat.

Even at the family level, this principle holds. Research on intergenerational wealth transfer shows that most inheritances erode not due to poor financial strategy, but due to weak emotional transmission. Families that do not model calm values—clarity, patience, stability—often fail to prepare heirs to steward capital effectively. Emotional endurance, not just legal planning, determines whether wealth sticks. In this way, the revolution extends beyond finance. It touches legacy, identity, even philosophy.

There is a reason why the subtitle of this book insists that staying calm beats getting rich quick. Not because speed is inherently bad, but because *unsustainable speed makes fragility inevitable.* When systems are constantly agitated, they break. When minds are always reactive, they lose discernment. When strategies are always shifting, they lose coherence. Calm endurance, by contrast, compounds. It turns time from an enemy into an ally. It lets the long arc of effort bend toward power.

And that brings us back to the central promise of this book: patience is not just a way to feel better about moving slowly—it is a way to *win differently.* To outlast, not outpace. To build what others won't wait for. To earn what others won't endure for. To hold what others will forfeit under pressure. That is the hidden wealth we now uncover—not with noise, but with discipline.

If that feels rare, that's because it is. And that rarity is the opportunity. Most of the market—financial, emotional, cultural—is still playing the short game. It rewards immediacy. That creates space for those willing to play the long one. Not with arrogance. Not with passive hope. But with precise, intentional, emotionally grounded strategy. The edge is no longer in knowing more. It is in *flinching less.* That is how you outlast. That is how you win. Quietly. Confidently. Without rushing.

The Final Question: Who Can You Become?

There is a moment—rare, often uncomfortable—when the pursuit of external achievement gives way to an internal reckoning. It usually arrives not during peak performance but in periods of quiet reflection. The market isn't moving. The inbox is empty. The adrenaline has faded. And there, beneath the layers of strategy, ambition, and activity, one question waits: *Who am I becoming through all of this?*

Modern life is designed to distract us from this question. Careers are increasingly gamified: titles, metrics, promotions. Businesses chase scale at the expense of clarity. Individuals are urged to accumulate, accelerate, optimise. In such a climate, identity is often mistaken for performance, and direction for velocity. The result is a pervasive but rarely articulated anxiety—not of failure, but of misalignment. *What if I'm climbing fast, but up the wrong wall?*

This subchapter asks a different question—not "What can you achieve?" but *Who can you become if you commit to the long game few are willing to play?* It is a reframing of success not as dominance, but as depth. Not as recognition, but as resilience. Not as accumulation, but as *transformation.* This is not a sentimental or moral argument. It is a practical one. Because the single most compounding asset in a lifetime—more than capital, connections, or credentials—is character. And character is not revealed by what we pursue quickly, but by what we endure patiently.

To reimagine yourself as a resilient builder rather than a competitor in a race requires dismantling the deeply embedded belief that life is zero-sum. That if others are ahead, you are behind. That if you pause, you fall. This narrative may produce bursts of motivation, but it undermines long-term development. A competitive identity is fragile because it is externally anchored. It relies on other people's timelines, milestones, and comparisons. But a builder's identity—one rooted in process, principle, and patience—compounds internally. It strengthens with time, not just with results.

This shift has serious implications for how we build careers. A competitor optimises for optics: prestigious roles, flashy outcomes, linear progression. A builder optimises for *optionality and integrity*—choosing paths that may look slower now but offer exponential leverage later. Take the example of someone who turns down a high-paying but soul-sapping role in favour of a less visible opportunity that allows them to master a rare skill. In year one, it may look like a mistake. In year ten, it may look like wisdom. *Builders tolerate being misunderstood temporarily in order to be unshakeable eventually.*

Resilience in the long game demands a particular kind of courage—not the courage to leap, but the courage to *wait without applause.* To refine without recognition. To double down on first principles even as the world trades them for short-term hacks. That discipline is what separates not just successful people from unsuccessful ones, but *aligned people from reactive ones.* It's the difference between being clever and being clear. Between chasing opportunities and *earning the ability to choose them.*

To be clear, this orientation is not about passivity. It is not about doing less. It is about doing *better over longer arcs.* This includes more precise choices, more honest conversations, and more deliberate refusals. It's about acting with the conviction that the most meaningful outcomes—personal, professional, financial—require *depth, not drama.* And depth requires time. But most people do not structure their lives to allow for depth. They are too busy signalling motion to actually *go anywhere meaningful.*

This is why the long game is rare—not because it is hidden, but because it is *psychologically expensive.* It demands that you live for delayed payoff in a world built around instant reaction. That you choose clarity over consensus. That you trade validation for sustainability. Most are not willing to make that trade. But those who are gain access to something the reactive world cannot offer: *a trajectory that is uniquely their own.*

That uniqueness is not found in grand vision boards or ambition statements. It is shaped daily—through decisions made in quiet hours, risks taken without guarantee, habits cultivated without hype. This is the emotional architecture of self-authorship. It doesn't come from asking "What should I do next?" but from asking *"Who do I need to become in order to do that well?"* That single shift reframes your development not as tactical, but transformational.

Consider the long arc of mastery in any field—investment, medicine, teaching, entrepreneurship. The first few years are often dominated by imitation. You mimic, borrow, execute. But something changes in the second decade. If you've endured—without burning out, selling out, or dropping out—you start to see things others miss. You make fewer, better moves. Your edge is not effort. It's discernment. *That evolution can't be fast-tracked.* It requires becoming someone who can carry not just knowledge, but *the emotional weight of insight.*

That insight is what allows you to make decisions others can't—because you're not reactive, you're calibrated. You don't just know the game. You know *how to play it on your terms.* This is why so many truly great investors, founders, and thinkers often peak late. Not because they lacked opportunity early on, but because it took time to *become someone capable of holding big outcomes without collapsing under them.* The world doesn't talk about that emotional dimension. But it is the foundation.

So what does it take to build this version of yourself? Not productivity systems. Not vision boards. Not willpower sprints. It takes *emotional compounding*: practices that stretch your capacity for boredom, discipline, perspective, and patience. The world tempts us with novelty. But mastery, identity, and reputation compound only when you stay long enough to see the returns *most people exit before earning.*

To ask yourself "Who can I become?" is not to abandon ambition—it is to root it in something more enduring than applause. It is to set your strategy not against the loudest voices, but against *the longest arc of who you are capable of becoming.* This is not easy work. It is not glamorous. But it is the difference between a life that flashes and fades, and a life that *builds the kind of gravity that attracts opportunity, trust, and clarity without chasing them.*

Every decision you make is a vote for the kind of self you are constructing. Do you say yes to what is urgent, or what is essential? Do you chase validation, or do you refine your competence quietly? Do you pivot to what is trending, or deepen your edge where others get bored? The long game isn't theoretical. It is *designed through the discipline of daily decisions.*

At some point, the question of "What am I doing with my life?" becomes insufficient. The more honest and productive question is: *"Who am I willing to become, slowly, deliberately, and without applause—so that I can hold, shape, and sustain what matters most?"* That question is your compass. It points not to quick wins, but to enduring identity. And the courage to ask it—and act on it—is the real mark of someone playing the long game.

The Emotional Wealth Practice

The rarest form of wealth in the modern world is not material—it is psychological. To remain calm while others panic, focused while others scatter, patient while others sprint, is not a matter of temperament alone. It is a cultivated capability. Emotional patience, as this book has argued, is not merely a personal virtue; it is a systemic advantage. It underlies good decision-making, sustained compounding, and integrity across decades. But like any form of wealth, emotional patience does not appear spontaneously. It is built. And what builds it is not theory, but practice.

Most people vastly overestimate the power of information and underestimate the role of *structure.* They collect insights without translating them into systems. They highlight ideas without creating habits to embody them. They feel inspired but not transformed. What's missing is not knowledge, but a *discipline for internal alignment*—a regular, deliberate pattern of thought and behaviour that hardens emotional patience into character.

This final subchapter presents an integrated practice—not a list of hacks, not a motivational mantra, but a sustainable approach to internal compounding. It is what transforms patience from a fragile intention into a resilient trait. Because it's one thing to *agree* with the idea that patience creates asymmetric outcomes. It's another to *live in such a way that it becomes second nature.*

Let us begin with a basic truth: emotional wealth does not come from reacting well during crises. It comes from *training for them when things are calm.* That training starts with managing attention. In a digital economy engineered to fracture your focus, reclaiming the capacity to *hold your mind steady* is foundational. Not because mindfulness is trendy, but because wealth-building decisions require *time-insensitive clarity.* If your attention is hijacked by urgency, your patience is neutralised before it begins.

The first anchor of emotional wealth, therefore, is attention hygiene. This includes boundaries around inputs—what you consume, when, and how often. It is nearly impossible to cultivate patience if you live in an environment of *constant stimulation and comparison.* The moment-to-moment volatility of social media, breaking news, or even market dashboards trains the brain into *micro-reactivity.* Emotional investors, reactive parents, impulsive entrepreneurs—they all share one common feature: *a broken relationship with stillness.*

A practice of emotional wealth starts here: creating predictable, low-noise spaces where long-form thinking can emerge. This is not romantic minimalism. It is neurological design. A calm brain sees further. And seeing further is the precondition for long-term action.

The second pillar is self-observation without judgment. Patience is often sabotaged not by external chaos, but by internal narratives.

"I'm behind." "It's too late." "I need to catch up." These thoughts don't reflect reality—they reflect *comparison-driven scripts* absorbed from cultural noise. The ability to observe one's inner dialogue, interrupt unhelpful patterns, and reframe decisions with perspective is a powerful tool of emotional leverage. Over time, this habit changes your baseline from *urgency to clarity.*

This requires more than occasional reflection. It requires a system—a recurring process of daily mental check-in. Many of the world's top performers across disciplines—from elite athletes to seasoned investors—keep *decision journals.* Not for nostalgia, but to *detect patterns of impulse and fear,* and adjust their internal calibration accordingly. When you track how you react over time, you start to distinguish between *perceived urgency and actual importance.* This is the ground on which emotional patience is trained.

The third practice is strategic inaction. This may sound paradoxical, but deliberate *non-doing* is not passivity—it is *composure with intent.* High performers often struggle with this. They associate value with movement, control with intervention. But the compounding effect of great decisions often depends on *what you don't do.* The businesses that scale are often those that *resist premature scaling.* The investors who thrive are those who *refuse to trade during noise.* The careers that endure are built by those who *don't pivot at every frustration.* Building in time to sit still, reassess, and do nothing when action is not required is a sign of *emotional leverage,* not laziness.

To make this a practice, you must ritualise it. Create protected windows—weekly, monthly, quarterly—where you review not just what you've done, but what you've *withheld from doing,* and why. This reflection embeds the conviction that *restraint is an asset.* Without this step, your environment will default you back into movement for its own sake.

The fourth element is values-based review. Emotional wealth is not about achieving calmness for its own sake. It is about aligning your actions with what *matters most over time.* This requires revisiting, refining, and recommitting to your *core principles* regularly. Too often, people misattribute emotional turmoil to external circumstances when it actually stems from *values drift*—the subtle but dangerous gap between what you're doing and what you truly believe.

An emotional wealth practice includes a quarterly or semi-annual values audit: Am I living and investing in accordance with my most enduring beliefs? Are my current pursuits congruent with the long arc of what I care about? This kind of intentional alignment restores inner coherence, which reduces cognitive friction. And reduced friction allows for *clearer, calmer, more durable execution.*

A fifth component is resilience conditioning. Patience is not passivity. It is endurance. And endurance needs practice under strain. Just as athletes use load and recovery to build physical resilience, emotionally wealthy individuals *train themselves under controlled emotional strain.* This might involve choosing to delay gratification, to sit with discomfort, or to challenge a limiting belief system—on purpose, and repeatedly. The more you *intentionally expose yourself to emotionally complex experiences*, the more robust your baseline becomes when true volatility arrives.

For example, high-integrity leaders often practise difficult conversations not when it's convenient, but as a regular muscle. Long-term investors review their thesis not just during up-markets, but when sentiment turns. Parents and mentors who shape others emotionally don't just protect from discomfort—they equip others to metabolise it. This is resilience not as slogan, but as *structure.*

To summarise this without simplification: emotional wealth is the *compounding result of structured stillness, strategic reflection, conscious restraint, values alignment, and voluntary resilience.* These are not reactive responses. They are proactive systems. They require no market permission, no economic environment, no permission slip from the world. Only a decision to *train yourself like a long-term thinker, not just to believe like one.*

Ultimately, emotional patience is not the avoidance of struggle. It is the ability to endure *with direction.* To stay steady in uncertainty not because you are indifferent, but because you are *internally ordered.* The most successful investors, builders, and thinkers do not eliminate risk or noise—they become the kind of people *for whom those things hold less sway.*

This is what the Emotional Wealth Practice is about: transforming patience from a theoretical ideal into a lived capacity. Not sporadically. But daily. If there is a final message to take from this book, it is this: your emotional landscape *is your investment portfolio.* What you reinforce internally—calm, conviction, discernment—directly shapes what you compound externally.

Emotional patience isn't just a behavioural trait. It is a systemic design. Build that system, and you don't just withstand volatility—you *outlast it with clarity.* That is the hidden return of this work. And it is always available to those disciplined enough to practise.

About the Author

Jonathan Mercer writes at the nexus of behavioral psychology, philosophy, and long-view financial strategy. With extensive research into decision-making under uncertainty, Mercer explores how emotional patience—not hustle—serves as the invisible architecture of lasting wealth. Through data-informed insights and evocative case studies, he offers readers a grounded, soulful roadmap to build not just wealth, but resilience. Outlast is his defining work—an invitation to reclaim calm, cultivate composure, and thrive through endurance.

www.ingramcontent.com/pod-product-compliance
Lightning Source LLC
Chambersburg PA
CBHW031347230926
51848CB00002B/426
* 9 7 8 9 3 7 1 7 7 1 1 6 0 *